REAL
SMARTS

Leveraging smartphones and new technologies
in your **Real Estate** Business

Marna Friedman

Real Smarts: Leveraging smartphones and new technologies in your Real Estate Business
Published by MWF Publishing, Dallas, GA

Other books by Marna Friedman
EVENTually Perfect
The Small Business That Could™
The Small Business That Could™ For Women
The Social Launch Toolkit

ISBN: 978-0-9840169-5-2
Library of Congress Control Number: 2012923362

Manufactured in the United States of America

Table of Contents

Symbol Key:

There are several items that I wanted to call out in this book.
They are each broken out into specific types of categories:

 Notes on technology

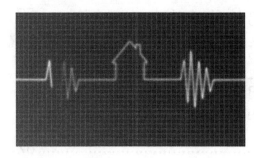 Definitions

 Real Estate Detail

Introduction

While speaking at a conference, I learned from the session attendees that they wanted a "one-stop" shop to learn how to use social media information:

What	What exists in social media
Where	Where can I find the applications
How	How do I use these applications to engage my community

The chapters of this book offer a basic framework of the different platforms available to Real Estate Agents and how to use them. There are links to a few different options that expand the functionality of the platforms for you to understand what's possible.

- Learn why technology can help you enhance the productivity of your business
- How your smartphone/tablet can become a "virtual" office
- How to leverage social media to engage, not sell, and grow your client base

NOTES

_____

_____

_____

_____

_____

Who is this book intended for?

I wrote this book for the Real Estate Agents just getting started in real estate or with technology. It's also for those businesses looking at investing in new technologies and wanting to understand them.

Much like a startup business, Real Estate Agents need to think about the ROI before investing in new technologies. Ask the questions. And consider the response. While a mobile app for your business is a nice thing to have, do you need it? Will your clients/community use it? Do you have the budget for it? Remember that real estate is usually about local, and only you can determine how to leverage technology for your community.

Cost of Tools

Many of the tools I discuss in this book are available at no cost or low cost. I am a firm believer that you should validate the need for technology before you invest in it. You wouldn't buy a car until you test drove it, so you shouldn't invest in social media applications until you try them.

What you will learn

This book is meant to be a guidebook of what's possible and what's available. It's an introduction to technology. You need to understand what's possible before you can begin to use it.

NOTES

_____

_____

_____

_____

_____

_____

Some caveats:
1. You can't be all things to all people. Pick one or two social media platforms to start to engage with your community.

2. Use your website as "home base". Update your blog frequently and share information with your community. Become the local "expert".

3. Research your options. Test. Validate.

4. Be careful. Once you place content on the internet, it is available to anyone.

5. Follow the rules. Ensure that you abiding by the rules and regulations of your company; as well as any local, city, state and federal regulations that may be in place.

Most of all, engage your community. Speak to them like they are sitting across from you. Have a conversation. Social media is all about engagement. Think about them. It is not about sales!

So read through the chapters of this book and determine where you want to participate. Create reasonable goals. Good luck!

NOTES

_____

_____

_____

_____

_____

NOTES

_____

_____

_____

_____

_____

_____

Why Technology

Learn how technology can help you build and grow your community while increasing the productivity of your business through:

- 📖 Integration of social media
- 📖 Engaging your community
- 📖 Increased productivity

Realtors need to embrace technology

As a realtor, embracing new technologies can help improve your productivity, engage your community and grow your business. Understanding all of these new technologies can also seem overwhelming. And while you may not be using social media, your customers probably are, learning about your business and others.

Some of the things you need to think about when using social media: credibility, integrity, authenticity and transparency.

NOTES

_____

_____

_____

_____

_____

Each of these characteristics impact the others. And to be viewed as an expert in your field, I believe you need to embrace all of them. That said, many of you will claim to be too busy to participate in social media. And subsequently hire someone to "do it" for you. The voice needs to be yours as does the message. And consistency is critical to your success. Having someone "help" you with social media is fine, but only after you have built your brand, established your message and found your voice. Then they can maintain the foundation you have built.

Navigating the technology by creating a roadmap

Understanding the technologies that are available and what they offer will help you decide which ones to use and how to integrate them into your real estate business. There is no perfect plan. Each person is different, and how you approach technol-

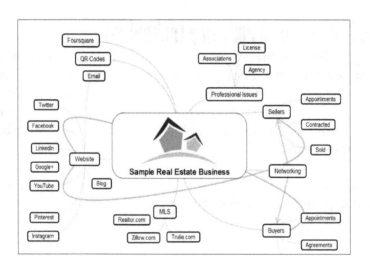

NOTES

_____

_____

_____

_____

_____

ogy will vary from others. A mindmap is a visual diagram of your business and can provide a "blueprint" of how all of these technologies come together in your business. Since you are a realtor, much of what you do is visual like helping a client stage a home. Creating a mindmap is a visual representation of how you can navigate technology.

Credibility

While you probably think that adding listings to your Facebook Page and tweeting about them validates you as a Realtor, it actually only validates you as a **sales**person. You gain credibility by sharing information. Knowing your community and being seen as an expert is how you gain a reputation as an expert. As people begin to look at listing their home or buying a new home, they typically want a realtor that truly understands what they want. Focus on helping local businesses become successful, promote someone else's business for free by blogging about

NOTES

_____

_____

_____

_____

_____

the great food at a local restaurant, or great service at a local retail shop – offer proof of your credibility. Sharing information openly and honestly enhances your credibility.

Integrity

While credibility is all about the "believability" of what you say, integrity is all about honesty. It also describes someone with strong moral principles. As you become active in social media, you need to think about who you are and how you want to be perceived.

Authenticity

A person who is authentic is true to their personality, spirit, or character. For this reason, I believe that individuals should develop their own brand and find their voice in social media. Similar to a conversation in a coffee shop, your comments on social media speak to your authenticity. So being authentic is about being genuine, removing the filters.

Transparency

Putting it all together, transparency is about honesty and being open. This includes what you see and how you respond to what others say.

Even though you want to be yourself in your approach to social media, you don't (and shouldn't) share everything. You are entitled to a personal life, but you need to set the barriers. Once you cross the line, you have opened the door for others. I made a decision long ago to keep my Facebook account personal, and

NOTES

_____

_____

_____

_____

while I have accepted invitations from people I work with, I consider them friends. It's your decision to make, and you need to be strategic.

Types of Technology

Many times when you speak about technology, people think about apps. Technology, as discussed in this book, can involve a website, social media, QR codes, location-based applications, and the list continues to grow daily.

- Learn why technology can help you engage your visitors
- Quickly launch a website
- Ability to update site content
- How to monitor your social media
- Social Media ROI
- How to navigate the different social media platforms

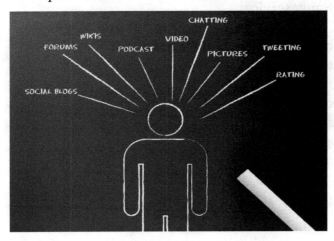

NOTES

_____

_____

_____

_____

_____

Websites

A website offers an online presence for your business, but it also provides a portal of sharing information and integrating your social media.

Social Media

If you aren't using Social Media to grow your community, you are missing an amazing opportunity. But along with this opportunity comes a commitment to that community. But you should also implement a social media policy to ensure the consistency of your company message, protect yourself and your company. The major reasons to have a published social media policy include:

- Protecting your company's reputation
- Protect your intellectual property
- Avoid confusion on legal issues
- Increase awareness of your company/brand
- Customer service

Learn about the different platforms and tools including:

- Twitter
- Facebook
- LinkedIn
- Pinterest
- Google+
- and more ...

NOTES

_____

_____

_____

_____

_____

Social Media Tools

While they may not truly be "tools", there are several items being used in social media that can help with your community engagement including:

- Location Based Apps
- QR Codes
- Badges

Email Campaign Tool

Using an email campaign tool to collect emails of those interested in your business is critical for follow-up and also for marketing in the future. As your list continues to grow, it becomes more valuable for your business and to others.

Applications

Smartphone and other applications expand your business reach beyond your website and social media. These apps help you integrate your current tools. As the technology has advanced, access to applications have become more economical.

As you navigate through the chapters of this book, you will begin to understand how to leverage technology for your real estate business.

NOTES

_____

_____

_____

_____

_____

Notes

_____

_____

_____

_____

_____

Getting Started With Social Media

Learn how to leverage social media in your real estate business.
- Using Twitter, Facebook, LinkedIn, Pinterest
- Leveraging video and photos with YouTube and/or Flickr

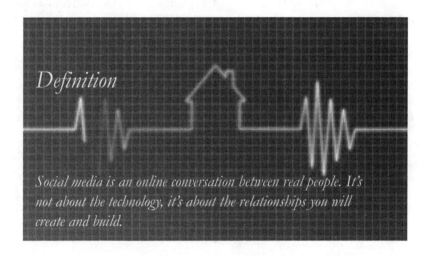

Definition

Social media is an online conversation between real people. It's not about the technology, it's about the relationships you will create and build.

NOTES

_____

_____

_____

_____

_____

Growing your community

Even though your website gives you an online presence, you need to augment it with social media. Not every social media application is right for your audience. Understanding how to use social media will help you to engage with your community.

Creating Your Social Media Persona

It's important to understand how social media can help with your business strategy. Before you begin to use social media, you need to register for the applications you want to use. Even though you may not use all of the applications listed below, you may want to register for an account to use in the future. If your user name is consistent, it is easier for your community to find you. A quick way to find out if the name you want is available is to use Namechk. This application will do a quick search of the name you select and let you know if it is available.

NOTES

_____

_____

_____

_____

You can type your username in the top box and click OK. Keep in mind that you should use a name that is less than 20 characters, especially since tweets from Twitter are only 140 characters. It's also easier to remember a shorter name. And since Twitter uses hashtags (which we will discuss later) this should not be the same as your Twitter name. The screen will quickly change to show you which sites have that username available, which names are taken, and also if there are domains with that username available. Clicking on each site will take you to the site, where you can register the name you have selected.

☐ Namchk
   http://namechk.com/
   check username availability at multiple social
   networking sites.

As you select the sites and register, be sure to remember your user ID and password.

According to Nielsen, almost 80% of the US internet users frequent social networks and blogs. And close to 40% of social media users access their sites on smartphones. But what does that mean to you?

NOTES

_____

_____

_____

_____

_____

Using Social Media

Most realtors include links to their social media on their marketing materials and property flyers. But that is not the same as "engaging" social media. Much like a conversation, if you aren't participating, you really aren't involved. And social media is not about your real estate business, it's about the community. You need to be involved with the conversation to engage potential clients - both buyers and sellers.

Social media communities are about engagement and not sales. While the real estate business tends to focus on sales, participation in social media offers an opportunity to join the conversation. The engagement can actually help to create and build relationships. Conversations on social media are indicative of what people want to talk about. Listening to these conversations creates ideas. Start conversations on different social media platforms to determine what people would want to learn more about, discuss, etc. But don't overwhelm your audience, start the conversation and wait for participation. Always remember that this is a conversation, not a sales pitch.

You can also create networking events so that your online community can meet in person. The earlier you start your networking events, the more opportunity you have to grow your community and increase your business. Invite your clients to participate in the community, they will become a representation of your ability to build relationships.

NOTES

_____

_____

_____

_____

Smartphone usage and statistics that realtors need to be aware of:

Statistics on REALTORS® and Technology[2]
- 38% of responding agents are looking at purchasing a smartphone
- 29% of responding agents are looking at purchasing an iPad
- 17% of responding agents are looking at purchasing a digital camera
- 35% of responding agents use an Adroid OS smartphone
- 28% of responding agents use an iPhone
- 18% of responding agents use a Blackberry
- 90.5% of REALTORS® use social media to some extent.

[2] http://www.realtor.org/field-guides/field-guide-to-quick-real-estate-statistics

NOTES

_____

_____

_____

_____

_____

Why Real Estate Agents Should Use Social Media

Statistics show that US consumers have spent $262 billion on-line so far this year, a 13.4% increase over all of 2012. This implies that more and more Americans are turning to the internet for purchasing decisions. So if everyone is playing in the same pond, how do you get noticed?

Become the resident expert. Remember that Real Estate is local. When people are looking to buy a home, they are usually looking at specific neighborhoods. Share information on your website about your area. And by sharing, I don't mean shouting from the rooftop that you have several listings in the neighborhood, I mean sharing information about the area. Is there a new restaurant you just visited? Tell us about it. How about the school activities? Did the students just win an award? Win a championship game? Perform a play?

Start a conversation on Facebook, send a tweet about an upcoming event. The more engaged you are in social media, the more people get to know you. And subsequently, will turn to you when buying or selling a home. You become the trusted advisor, the "friend" in the business. Conversely, if all you do is announce new listings and share real estate industry information, I would be looking for the mute button!

Are you starting to see how this works? Social media is all about being social. And if your peers are shouting from the rooftops, don't follow them! Think about the social events you attend.

NOTES

Don't you want to join the conversation? The blowhard is the one everyone is walking away from.

Some interesting statistics from the 2013 Social Media Industry Report:

- Facebook and LinkedIn are the two most important social networks for marketers, yet when forced to select one 49% chose Facebook
- 37% of marketers (slightly more than one in three) think that their Facebook efforts are effective
- As more and more businesses become social, those who best engage will stand out
- More than half of the respondents who have been using social media for at least 3 years report it has helped them improve sales
- Outsourcing social media management dropped from 30% in 2012 to only 26% this year

Those spending at least 6 hours per week on social media:

- 92% indicated increased exposure for their business
- 64% see lead generation benefits
- Nearly half saw a benefit of reduced marketing
- At least 60% saw improvements in search engine rankings

There are several more insights available, and the entire report can be found here:
HTTP://WWW.SOCIALMEDIAEXAMINER.COM/SOCIAL-MEDIA-MARKETING-INDUSTRY-REPORT-2013/

NOTES

_____

_____

_____

_____

_____

Creating a Social Media Strategy

As you begin to create your social media strategy it is important to understand:

- Social media is not about selling. No where in the terminology does it say sell. The focus is on social, and that translates to building relationships.
- Don't start using social media because "everyone else is doing it."
- Social media is a long-term commitment and requires dedication.

Creating a social media strategy will help you develop clear goals and objectives that mirror those of your business, while helping you build relationships.

Step 1: Goals and Objectives

What do you want to achieve with social media? Think **SMART**:

- **Specific**. Your goals need to be detailed so that you can determine whether you've achieved them or not.
- **Measurable**: You should be able to quantify goals with a numeric benchmark and they measure engagement, not sales.
- **Achievable**: Create measurable benchmarks that are realistic and based on what you've accomplished in the past. Don't count numbers.
- **Relevant**: If they don't relate to your objectives, it doesn't matter if you've achieved them.
- **Time Based**: Define the timeframe over which you'll achieve these goals.

NOTES

_____

_____

_____

_____

_____

It's also critical to know who you want to reach. Potential clients may not become clients for years, but if they are engaged in your community, they may refer other clients to you. Don't think of everyone as a client, but as a member of your community. As your community grows, so will your business.

Step 2: I Spy

Instead of jumping into the social media pool with both feet, play in the sandbox first. Look at what your competition is doing, listen to what others in your community are saying. Do a bit of research. Identify the influencers and engage with them. This is not only an opportunity to learn what to do, but also what not to do. You will probably see other realtors doing things that you may not feel comfortable doing. If it doesn't feel right, it probably isn't.

Step 3: Something To Talk About

Subscribe to blogs in your industry and create a list of industry influencers. Create lists on Twitter to follow their conversations and share. Engage with them so that they begin to know who you are. Much like new friendships, as you get to know each other, the relationship will become stronger. And when you are ready to become actively involved in social media, they will be there to engage with you and share your content.

Step 4: Join the Conversation

Participate in the conversations. Post comments on blogs, fo-

NOTES

_____

_____

_____

_____

_____

rums, retweet their tweets, answer questions on LinkedIn, participate in community groups on LinkedIn. As you become more engaged, you will see your own community grow as people now want to follow you. You begin to become an influencer in your community.

Step 5: Strengthen Relationships

Your business is about personal relationships between you and your clients. And as you become more engaged on social media, it's sometimes easy to get lost in the conversation. But IRL (in real life) is critical to your success. So attend local events to network and strengthen relationships. Remember to "merge" your offline and online relationships to grow your network and business even more.

Step 6: Measure Results

Your time is valuable, and you want to make sure you are using it wisely. And since social media is about being social, sometimes it is difficult to put a monetary value on it. But you still have to consider the ROI (return on investment). Many social media tools will offer you analytics and insight tools to measure your engagement, which will help you determine if they are the right platforms for you, and you are utilizing them successfully.

- *Don't be swayed by numbers*
  It's not about how many followers you have on Twitter, or fans on your Facebook page. It's about how you are engaging with them. How many comments on

NOTES

_____

_____

_____

_____

_____

your blog posts, number of times you are mentioned in blogs and forums, how many people have read what you wrote

- *What's your online reputation*
  While you want to be mentioned, are the comments positive? Online reviews and testimonials are every-where. Are you monitoring what is being said and responding to the good, and the bad.

- *Forging partnerships*
  Identify relationships where they may be opportunities that might benefit your benefit. Think about the part-nerships you already have and identify those in your network that mirror those partnerships. For example, home repairs, insurance, attorneys, etc.

- *Don't neglect your website*
  As you become more involved with social media, you may forget your website. Create content on your website and share it on social media. But make sure redirect your social media community to your website. That's where your listings are, where your buyer/seller information is, and all of the great information about you. If they don't get there, they won't know.

Step 7: Analyze the Results, and Modify the Game Plan

Your social media strategy doesn't end with measurement, it's part of the process. Use the analytics to help you under-stand what's working, what's not working and where you can

NOTES

_____

_____

_____

_____

_____

improve your efforts. And remember that you can't do it all, none of us can. Select the platforms that work best for you, where you feel most comfortable. Because that's where you will achieve the most success. But as you continue to become more comfortable, you need to move beyond your comfort zone, so that you can continue to engage more people and grow your community. As you review the analytics, you will determine the best time and days to engage.

The most important thing to remember is that in relationship-building, it takes commitment. If you aren't ready to make that commitment, don't. Because it takes time and commitment to be successful in social media.

NOTES

_____

_____

_____

_____

_____

Popularity Has Its Benefits

Learn how to become popular
- Finding the influencers
- Becoming a subject matter expert

Understanding how to leverage social media

Social media experts have frequently discussed the importance of listening and engaging with others. The key is to find the right people to listen to and engage with. Much like a conversation with others, you want to make sure that the people you are talking to are actively engaged. How much of an influence do they have over their audience, and your audience?

One of the easiest ways to get started with social media is to listen. As you continue to develop your online presence reach out to the people in your community. They can be subject matter experts, local businesses, local officials, peers, employees or others. Subscribe to their blogs, follow them on Twitter. When you feel comfortable, join the conversation. Repeat what they say by retweeting them on Twitter, or sharing their information

NOTES

_____

_____

_____

_____

_____

on your Facebook page.

Even though you may think this is time consuming, remember that it takes time to build relationships. There are also tools that can help you.

☐ Followerwon
http://followerwonk.com/

☐ Topsy
http://topsy.com/

☐ Twellow
http://www.twellow.com/

You can also search Twitter itself to find out "what's happening, right now, with the people and organizations you care about." Just type a keyword in the search bar at the top, and a stream of tweets will appear on that topic. And as you continue to build your social media community, you might want to create lists to help you. List building within Twitter is easy.

Popularity is an important part of many people's value systems and engaging the right people can influence your reputation.

NOTE: *unlocking a technology tidbit for you*

NOTES

_____

_____

_____

_____

_____

Becoming an Influencer

As you become more comfortable with social media, you may want to become an influencer. Much like becoming a subject matter expert, becoming an influencer on social media can impact your business.

Where should you participate?

There are so many platforms, how do you determine where to become actively involved. You need to go back to the beginning. Where are the influencers in your business? Have you engaged them and shared your own information with them? One way to become engaged on Twitter is to participate in a "chat" on your topic of choice. A chat enables you to share your opinions and experiences with others that have similar interests.

Real Estate Detail

A list of the top social media Twitter chats can be found at http://socialfresh.com/twitter-chats.

You can search this wiki by subject for chat that is relevant to your business:
http://www.gnosisarts.com/home/Tweetchat_Wiki/By_Subject

NOTES

_____

_____

_____

_____

_____

Participating in a Twitter Chat also helps you prepare to lead your own chat. As you become more comfortable with a chat, you will become more involved. You also want to become familiar with tools that can help you participate, and possibly lead, a chat.

Where can you gain credibility?

Your credibility will usually grow as your visibility grows, as long as you are authentic in your social media activity. Identifying where your influencers participate, as well as where your community is will help to determine your platform(s). As Twitter, Facebook and LinkedIn continue to hold steady as the top 3 most popular social media platforms, Pinterest and Google+ are quickly gaining traction.

Google+ reached 50 million users in 3 months compared to Twitter, Facebook and LinkedIn. And as discussion about Google+ grows, it appears that it is an important place for businesses to participate. On Google+ you can search for conversations, on Facebook your search will result in pages or people. As with its search engine, Google+ places content search first rather than friends and/or pages. The platform also suggests people who are interested in that topic to include in your circles.

NOTES

_____

_____

_____

_____

How do you share information?

Beyond social media platforms, you should share content. As discussed earlier, you can create content and/or curate content. Either way, you attain a level of subject matter expert because you create it, or know where to find it. Use your participation on social media to gain insight into what your community is interested in. Take notes and create a calendar of ideas. Leave space for spontaneity. Listen to what people say, but also listen for what they are asking. Sometimes the questions go unspoken, but present the biggest opportunity.

How do you know if anyone's interested?

Offer your community an opportunity to participate in the conversation. On your website you should offer share buttons to share the content on other platforms, and the ability to comment on what they have read. And as they comment, you should respond to keep the engagement moving forward. You can also use StatCounter to monitor actual human activity on your website in real-time.

NOTES

_____

_____

_____

_____

_____

NOTES

_____

_____

_____

_____

_____

Facebook

Learn how to leverage Facebook in your real estate business.
- 📖 Why you should have a Facebook Page
- 📖 Creating a Facebook Page for your business
- 📖 Using Facebook Tabs
- 📖 Using Facebook Boost and Ads
- 📖 Understanding Facebook Analytics

Facebook is basically about friends and family. As you share information, you will continue to grow your Facebook community. But you need to determine if your community is on Facebook. You can also advertise through Facebook Ads, and if your community is active on Facebook, a Facebook page might provide a decent ROI.

Some of the questions you need to answer are:
- Are your customers on Facebook?
- Can you engage visitors in a conversation?
- Does Facebook offer a community for your business?
- Will your fan base grow based on content?

NOTES

_____

_____

_____

_____

_____

Why You Should Have A Business Page

While social media is about engagement, some of your personal friends and family members may not want to share information with your Real Estate community. As a business, you can share information and engage on your Facebook Page, which while managed through your Facebook account, is separate from your personal information. This keeps your personal life private, and I know for me, this is a very important factor. You can also control the privacy settings on your personal page and optimize publicity for your Business Page.

In addition, Facebook caps the amount of friends you can have on your personal profile page at 5,000, while your Business Page can have an infinite number of friends. As a business, you can have unlimited "friends", so as your business and engagement grows, so does your Business Page.

Real Estate Detail

You should carefully consider every friend request on your Facebook account, because friend requests are for your personal account. You do not have to "accept" the people who like your Business Page.

NOTES

_____

_____

_____

_____

Some other reasons to have a Facebook Business Page:

1. **SEO**

   Facebook Business Pages are indexed, like your website pages, which means that some of the public content may be indexed as well. While you want the SEO results to direct traffic to your website first, having a social presence is also very important. And you can add your Facebook page to your website as well.

2. **TAG IT**

   Depending on your personal page privacy settings, only friends can tag images, but on your Business Page any visitor can tag your images, as long as you have offered this option in your Business Page privacy settings. And since social media is about engagement, this is a positive result.

3. **TABS**

   This function is only available on Business Pages. You can offer links to other social media platforms through the Tabs on your Business Page, including Pinterest, YouTube, Flickr and more.

4. **ANALYTICS**

   Once you have 30 friends on your Business Page, you will receive analytics through Facebook insights.

5. **ADS**

   Increase awareness and engagement through Facebook Ads. Facebook advertising can be expensive, but it is

NOTES

_____

_____

_____

_____

_____

also very targeted offering a more effective option than a landing page. You can also promote your Business Page through ads, but not your personal page.

6. **CONTESTS**
   Facebook contests are often seen in tabs, and as we noted in #3, these are only available in Tabs. Contests build engagement which is the objective of social media.

7. **EVENTS**
   You can promote Open Houses through your Facebook Business Page to your community.

As you can see, there are several reasons to create a Business Page. The next few pages will take you through setting up your page.

Creating a Facebook page:

1. Go to your Facebook account, and click on Pages.

2. The option for "MORE" will pop up on the right of the Pages menu, and a new center screen will appear. Click on Create Page.

3. Select your type of business from the options provided. Since your Real Estate business is a local business, you should probably select the first option.

NOTES

_____

_____

_____

_____

_____

4. Complete all of the required information and click on Get Started. The next screen will produce a series of tabs to complete the necessary information about your business. Navigate through the tabs and complete all of the information.

5. PAY ATTENTION! The fourth option is to create an Ad. You have the option to create an ad or skip this page. Make the selection that best fits your needs/budgets.

6. A pop up window will appear asking you to invite your email contacts. This option will give Facebook access to your email list. You can select this option or click Next to move on.

7. The next steps will be about creating the "appearance" of your page. You should create your images so that you can quickly place them. The next few pages include Facebook Page layout and image sizes. The two most important to get started are:

   Facebook Cover photo: 851 x 315
   Facebook Profile photo: 180 x 180

NOTES

_____

_____

_____

_____

_____

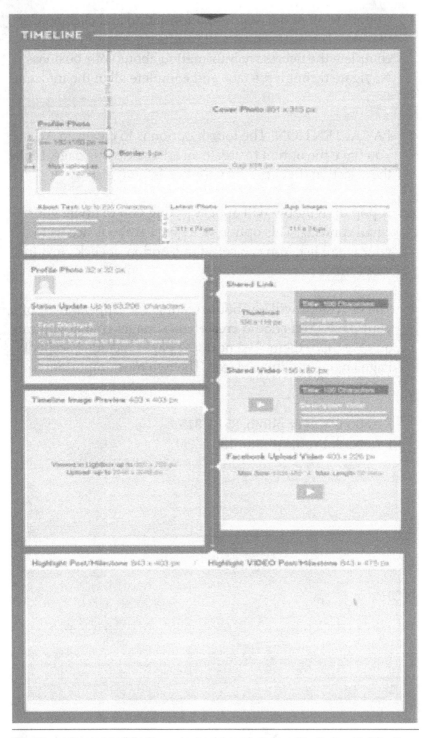

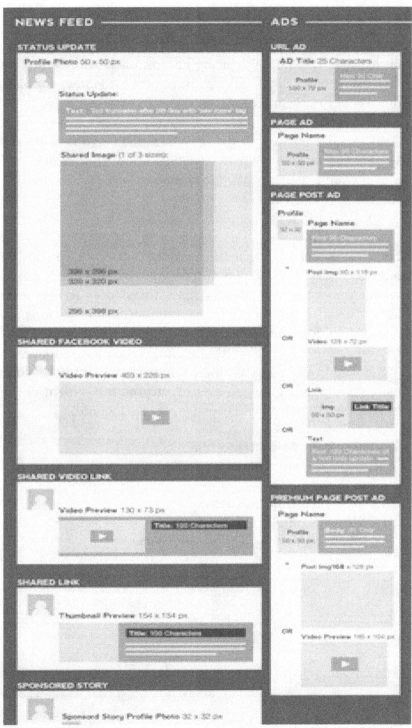

Using Facebook Tabs

Once you create your Facebook page, you will be able to use the tabs feature. The default tabs are Photos, Likes and Events. As a real estate agent, you will also have tabs for Homes for Sale, Your Agent Profile and more.

When you click on any of your tabs, you will see the above screen, which enables you to select the tab you want to edit, and add information to it.

You can also add tabs.

There are several tab applications available that you can add to your Facebook Page. Depending on your website, there might even be an option to "feed" your listings to your Facebook Page. Several of these options have financial implications, so you need to determine if they are worth the investment. You can also create a "wishlist" that includes the applications you have looked at and purchase them when you have built up your business enough to give you a return on your investment. Some of the applications you can use in your tabs include:

- [ ] Facebook Apps Marketplace
  https://apps.facebook.com/marketplace
- [ ] IDX Pro
  http://www.idxpro.com
- [ ] Realtor.com
  http://marketing.realtor.com/social

NOTES

_____

_____

_____

_____

_____

- ☐ Real Buzz
  http://www.real-buzz.com/facebookapps
- ☐ TopTab App
  http://toptabapp.com

Homes for Sale

There are applications that enable you to use a tab to your Facebook page and add listings to it.

- ☐ IDX Buzz
  http://www.idx-buzz.com/
- ☐ PX Agent
  http://pxagent.proxiopro.com/
- ☐ ReCake
  https://www.recake.com/
- ☐ Zillow
  http://www.zillow.com/webtools/facebook-apps/

Events

If your client has approved internet marketing, you might want to think about promoting Open Houses on Facebook. This will quickly make your community aware and increase the exposure for your event.

Contests

Another way to use Facebook is for contests and giveaways. Many of these applications have a cost and would need to be included your event or company budget. Creating a contest should include community involvement to help you engage

NOTES

_____

_____

_____

_____

with your "fans" and share information. Some contest applications include:

- ☐ Bulbstorm
  http://www.bulbstorm.com
- ☐ Social Prize
  http://socialprize.com
- ☐ Poll Everywhere
  http://www.polleverywhere.com
- ☐ TopTab Contest Application
  http://tabtabapp.com

Using Facebook Boost and Ads

While Facebook itself is a free platform, it has several different monetization strategies. And one of their recent additions is "boosted posts". Available on Business Pages, it's an option that enables you to purchase the right to be *boosted* in timelines and increase the number of eyes that see your posts, without inundating your hardcore fans with repetitive messaging.

Step 1
To boost a post, you will need to have at least 30 likes on your page.

Step 2
Share a post or update on your Page. Once you update your page, you will see the Boost Post on the bottom right of your update.

NOTES

_____

_____

_____

_____

_____

Step 3
Select Boost Post and your option screen will appear.

You can select the options that are appropriate for your business. If you select the second audience, you will have more options to narrow down your reach and better target your audience. And you can also set your maximum budget to boost your post. Facebook offers you the ability to select a location, certain ages, gender and location.

Once you have completed all of your options and agreed to Facebook's Terms & Advertising Guidelines, your post will be boosted. And you will be able to measure the results on your dashboard. The last column of your posts dashboard is promotion, and this pertains to your boost post campaign.

Facebook Ads

Facebook Ads can be used to advertise your business, listings, and special programs you may be offering. Similar to boosting your posts, you can target your audience and determine your maximum budget. One of the best features of Facebook Ads is that one campaign can contain several ads, each targeted to a different audience. For example, you can advertise your business through multiple ads with one to reach sellers and get listings, and another for buyers. Facebook Ads offers you the ability to target your ads with area, age, keywords, or other demographic information. And the ad analytics enable you to measure the results.

NOTES

_____

_____

_____

_____

_____

As you begin to set up your Facebook Ad, you will want to make notes of specifics for future campaigns, so you can prepare ahead of time.

- Ad Headline   25 characters
- Advertising Text   135 characters
- Ad Image   100 pixels wide x 72 pixels tall

Advertising Budget

You only pay for the clicks, known as number of impressions (CPM). The amount you pay will never be more than your daily or lifetime budget and there are no additional fees associated with your ad. So once you determine what you want to spend on your campaign, you can narrow it down to your daily or lifetime amount to launch the campaign.

Understanding Facebook Analytics

Facebook recently updated their Insights to offer page owners more information on what is working, what's not working and where there are opportunities for improvement. As you become more familiar with the metrics, you will be able to quickly determine how to improve engagement.

Once you use the analytics, you will be able to see what type of content receives the most engagement, shares and comments. And you may also be able to determine what content does not promote engagement. The sample Insights panel above shows you that the post reach is down, so you would look to see what you posted last week that received great response, or if you just

NOTES

_____

_____

_____

_____

_____

didn't post as much content this week as last.

The data above can be viewed when you click on an individual post. You can also drill down to each individual post to get a better insight into its reach. And as you can see, you also receive negative feedback, which can help in improving content.

Searching Facebook

As the real estate industry continues to embrace social media, they can become creative in how they use it. Like searching on the internet, and Twitter, you can search Facebook to find out what is being said in "public posts".

Other ways you can leverage Facebook for your real estate business include:

- Sharing homeowner information through videos and advertising like YouTube, webinars, etc.
- Local business news
- Local area updates - festivals, new business, school, etc.
- Information that is relevant and engaging to your community

NOTES

_____

_____

_____

_____

_____

NOTES

_____

_____

_____

_____

_____

 Google+

Learn how to leverage Google+ in your real estate business.
- 📖 Why you should have a Google+ Page
- 📖 Creating a Google+ Page
- 📖 Using Google+
- 📖 Google Authorship
- 📖 Using Google Hangouts

Why you should have a Google+ Page

While many people think of Google as the search engine, they provide several applications that real estate agents should be using. Google Plus is their social media platform. And there are several reasons you should be using it, including:

- Google Authorship attribution tags that link to websites and blog posts which can help your SEO
- Creating circles for different audiences including current and past clients, future prospects, industry partners, industry experts, competition and more
- Uploading correctly tagged images and videos to your profile
- Sharing content links that validate you as a real estate expert within your local area

NOTES

_____

_____

_____

_____

_____

- Engage with your partners to +1 content for quick indexing of your content
- Utilize the 'explore navigation' for keyword search
- Create events using Google+
- Writing and receiving authentic Google+ reviews

Create a Google+ Page

If you have already registered your business with Google, you probably have a Google+ presence that needs to be converted to a business page. If not, here is how you can create the page:

1. Go to Google+ to create your page:
   http://www.google.com/+/business/

2. Click on the blue button at the top right corner to create your page.

3. Select Local Places. And a popup will appear for you to complete. If your phone number is not already in Google, you will be asked to add it or not.

4. Since you selected Local Places, you will need to add an address for your business. This is typically the Broker's office that you work for.

5. All of this information will be populated into Google Maps as well to make it easier for potential clients to find you.
6. Agree to the Terms & Conditions to create your Google+

NOTES

_____

_____

_____

_____

_____

Business Page.

7. The next step would be to customize your page and add some contact information. Once you have completed this step, you should add a link to your Page on your website.

Using Google+

Some of the things you can do right away with your new Google+ Page:

1. Create a Local Google citation to show the actual business location and ensure that you have accurately posted your name, address and phone number of your business in all the local directories and that they have listed the information in exactly the same way. Any inaccuracies can result in an impact on your SEO rankings.

2. Some social media platforms are blocked at work, and this typically does not include Google+ as it is part of the Google suite of applications. So you can quickly interact with the people in your circles all day to share information, schedule Google Hangouts, and more.

3. Engage. As people in your circles share information, engage with them by making comments on their updates. This is a quick way for them to "see" you and learn who you are. And the SEO implications of Google+ means that people who interact with you are more likely to see your content in their search results.

NOTES

_____

_____

_____

_____

_____

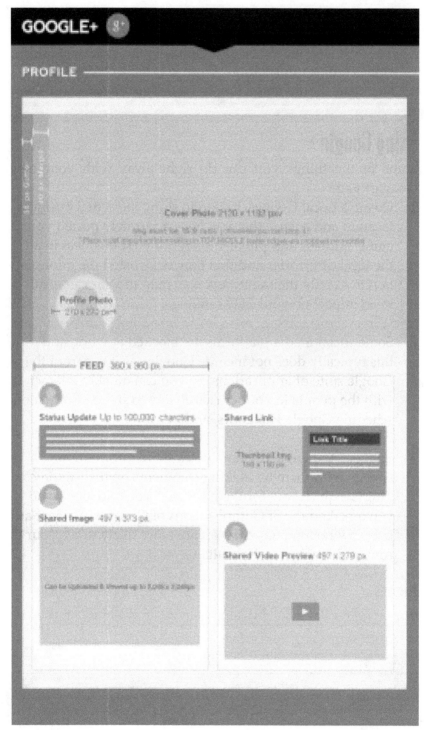

Google Authorship

In my opinion, Google+ is the best place for content marketing and sharing. Why? Because unlike content on the other platforms, your content on Google+ is automatically shared across the other Google platforms. But unless you are actually creating new content and expanding your circles, this won't necessarily work for you.

Regardless of how often you create new content, you should ensure that it is linked to your Google+ profile and that you have activated Google Authorship. Google Plus authorship can provide you with a higher visual profile in search results. And while Google+ content is treated the same way any other page is on Google, recent studies have shown that those who use Google authorship tend to average a higher Page Rank than those who do not and have more clicks on their content. So why would you not do this?

How to setup Google Authorship:
1. Once you have completed your Google+ Page setup as explained on page 43, go to your Google+ Page and click on **Home**.
2. Select **Profile** from the menu on the left.
3. Now click on **About** from *within* your profile.
4. Scroll down to **Links** on the right hand side.
5. Click **Edit** to add more to the *Other Profiles* section, i.e., Twitter, Facebook, LinkedIn, etc.
6. Move down to the next section of Links - **Contributor** -

NOTES

_____

_____

_____

_____

_____

and add your website and any additional websites that you contribute content to, i.e., guest blogger, etc.

7. Finally, go to the next section **Links**, and add your website.
8. Scroll down and click on SAVE.
9. You also need to *communicate* by adding the "rel=author" tag to your site which will help Google+ associate your content with your profile. We will review how to complete this on a WordPress website. So login to your dashboard and scroll down to users and select your profile.
10. Scroll down to the box labeled Google+ and paste your Google+ Page URL in the box. Click Update.
11. At this point, you probably want to confirm that you have done everything we said. To confirm that you have successfully completed the steps, go to Google's Rich Snippet tool (http://www.google.com/webmasters/tools/richsnippets) and test your website url. You should see your profile.

Mpressive Solutions LLC Business Strategies and Leveraging ... ⑦
mpressivesolutions.com/ ▾
by Marna Friedman - in 138 Google+ circles
Worth her weight in gold, **Marna Friedman** is fantastic! Her consultation fee is minimal compared to the wealth of information she will throw at you. I am so excited ...

Monitor your own search results over the next few weeks and you should quickly see that your content will appear in the format above. And as you continue to add new content, you will begin to reap the benefits of Google Authorship and enjoy the engagement.

NOTES

_____

_____

_____

_____

_____

Remember that Google+ is one part of Google applications. Google's VP of Product has stated:

> *"Google Plus is Google itself. We're extending it across all that we do — search, ads, Chrome, Android, Maps, YouTube — so that each of those services contributes to our understanding of who you are."*

Using Google Hangouts

Google Hangouts are video calls that enable you to meet without everyone having to be in the same place. You can meet clients that are interested in your area before they arrive. You can also host Hangouts with past clients to check in with them and "see" how they are doing. And sometimes you are just too busy to get to the office, but with a Google Hangout you can meet over your laptop. The caveat to Hangouts is that it is video. Unlike phone conversations, people can see you, where you are and how you look. So scheduling a call from the park is probably not a good idea.
in real time.

You can also see other public Hangouts scheduled by people in your circles. Try to make a point to join them and then engage with them. This helps to expand your community.

NOTES

_____

_____

_____

_____

_____

How to host a Hangout

1. Go to the home screen of Google+. In the right sidebar, you should see the Hangouts section. Click on the green "Start a hangout" button.

2. Create a Hangout and invite some people. You might want to test this out with friends and family before you schedule it with a client. Learn how to use the technology and become comfortable with it before you include it in your business tools.

If you are anything like me, you will find that you will be able to develop stronger relationships on Google+ that are more relevant to business than the ones you develop on Facebook. Having the right expectations of your different social networks helps to make the experience more beneficial. While I share some of the same content on Google+ that I share on my Facebook page, I find that since it is business focused and educational, it garners more engagement on Google+.

But you need to decide which platforms are the right ones for you. And as I have said before, like any new relationship, start by listening and learning, move on to engagement and then make and grow new relationships.

NOTES

_____

_____

_____

_____

_____

LinkedIn

Learn how to leverage LinkedIn in your real estate business.
- Your LinkedIn Profile
- Building Your LinkedIn Network
- LinkedIn Groups

LinkedIn is a valuable tool for connecting with like-minded professionals. You can quickly create a group on LinkedIn and begin to have discussions on relevant topics. Building a community on LinkedIn offers an opportunity to share information and ask questions of decision-makers who in turn can support your brand and your business.

Your LinkedIn Profile

You are your business. And your profile is you. So you need to make sure that it is current and accurate. Depending on your background, you can use your own discretion in how far you go back. But remember that people want to know about you, and quickly recognize your area of expertise.

NOTES

_____

_____

_____

_____

_____

Steps in completing your profile

1. **Create a relevant headline**
   While your complete profile won't be seen by every-one, but your headline will. And if you want to be found by people in your industry, you need to include the words that related to your industry. So if you are a real estate agent, realtor, real estate broker, etc., put it in your headline.

2. **Spell check and grammar**
   How many times have you read a profile with spell-ing errors and formed an opinion of that person? You definitely don't want to be them. Hold yourself to the same standards. Spelling and grammatical errors send a negative message and one that can hurt your reputa-tion.

3. **It's all about you - or is it?**
   Just like online review sites, clients and customers will research all they can about you. They'll look for com-mon interests, reasons to use you over another person, determine if you are "qualified" to be their real estate agent. And potential partners may be looking for you as well. Review your profile as though you were them, would you hire you? Do you have tenured experience?

4. **Stand out from the crowd**
   Each of us is unique, and we have different strengths and personalities. Much like applying for a job, why should a client hire you? How do you stand out from

NOTES

_____

_____

_____

_____

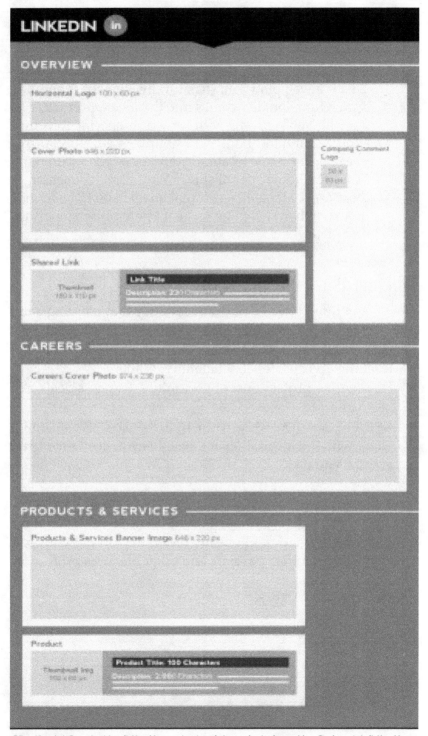

the crowd? Even though LinkedIn is a professional platform, you need to stand out in order to be chose

5. **Optimization**
   This is a web platform, so naturally, keywords and search functionality comes into the mix. Optimize your LinkedIn profile with keywords specific to your expertise and location. For example, if you specialize in a specific resort location, your keywords would be "vacation home specialist Key West Florida. Each of these are searchable terms that enable you to be found quickly when searching for real estate professionals in that area.

Building Your LinkedIn Network

How many times have I heard someone say that building a real estate business is about building relationships through your network? Well, LinkedIn is about:

- Building your professional identity online
- Discovering professional opportunities, business deals, and new ventures
- Learning about news in your industry and around town, along with the inspiration and insights you need to be great at what you do.

Now that you have created your profile, you should connect with people. Find former co-workers that don't know about your new career, and might be interested in working with you. Connect with mentors, partners and other business profession-

NOTES

_____

_____

_____

_____

_____

als that you have met along the way. As you continue to build your network, you will begin to reconnect and connect with others as well. But like other social media platforms, this is not about numbers, but about networking.

LinkedIn is a great tool for residential and commercial real estate professionals to build relationships that lead to sales. But leveraging LinkedIn to grow your business takes time. Some of the ways you can use LinkedIn include:

1. **Recommendations.** Typically the people you connect with on LinkedIn are the people who know you professionally and can attest to your character, professional ethics, and business acumen. And this translates to the fact that LinkedIn recommendations are equivalent to testimonials. And since we have already established that building relationships and growing your network is critical to your career, LinkedIn recommendations can become an important part of your profile.

2. **Company Page**. Unlike other social media platforms, your personal profile on LinkedIn can be *linked* to your Company Page. This means that if you own the Company or work for a firm, you should link your profile to that page. This automatically gives you double exposure. So if someone is looking at your Company Page and all of the people on it, you have just as much possibility to be the person they contact as anyone else on the page.

3. **Groups**. While most people would tend to join Groups of like- minded professionals, you should remember that this is about building relationships and growing your business.

NOTES

_____

_____

_____

_____

_____

Connecting on LinkedIn:

On LinkedIn, the people who are part of your network are called your *connections*. Connections, by the mere term, implies that you are connected. And there are multiple levels of connections on LinkedIn, which we will discuss later. To *make* a connection, you need to:

1. Find the person you want to connect with on LinkedIn.
2. Click Connect next to their name.
3. From the drop down menu, select how you know the person. Be honest - it speaks to your credibility. If you are asked for additional information and don't have it, then you probably don't really know the person well enough to connect - yet.
4. If you met them at a networking event, you should have a business card with contact information that will enable you to select Other and input their email. **Always** include a note reminding the person how you know each other and why you would like to connect. Be brief, characters are limited.
5. Click **Send Invitation**.
6. Once they receive your invitation, they can choose to accept your invitation, or not.
7. When they accept your invitation, you are now a direct connection. LinkedIn describes this connection as being one degree away from you on the LinkedIn network.
8. You will see that your LinkedIn network will show you how many people are in your network, and how many people that connects you to in the entire LinkedIn Net-

NOTES

_____

_____

_____

_____

_____

work. All of these numbers will grow exponentially since as you increase your connections, you increase the number of people in your network because you are 2-4 connections away from everyone in the network.

YOUR LINKEDIN NETWORK

713 Connections link you to
16,943,912+ professionals

24,666 New people in your
Network since July 26

LinkedIn Groups

As a savvy real estate professional, you know that the more people you connect with, the bigger your reach. And by joining LinkedIn groups in your demographic area, you are automatically connected to every other member of that group. But being a member of group doesn't guarantee a *connection*. You need to participate in group discussions, share information and build relationships. Another benefit of groups is that you can quickly identify people in your geographic area that might be good leads.

You are limited to 50 groups, which seems like a lot, but you will discover that you will reach that number quickly. So be strategic. While you want to join groups where you can leverage your real estate business, you should also think about networking with other professional groups that can share skills

NOTES

_____

_____

_____

_____

and resources with you to help you grow your business.

It's easy to search for Groups by keywords, location, and more.

1. Log into LinkedIn.
2. Type Groups in the search box and click the search icon.
3. Type search words in the search box, i.e., County you work in, real estate and hit enter
4. Be mindful of the number of members, how many of the members are already in your network, how many discussions are listed - these can all be indications of how active the group is. But another way is to review the group's statistics. You can select a group, and once on their page select the **more** option from the menu and scroll down to Group Statistics. You'll be able to see group demographics, growth and activity. Scroll through the options and view the information to determine if the group is a good selection for you.
5. Participate in discussions. Share information without selling. This is not about sales, it's about building relationships.

Direct Connections vs Group Connections

Direct connections should be people you know and trust. It is not advisable to add strangers to your network or accept invitations from people you don't know. Group connections on the other hand are automatically connected to you through the group. As you build relationships in Groups, some of the members may become direct connections by inviting you to join their network. Again, be careful that you don't accept invitations from strangers.

NOTES

_____

_____

_____

_____

_____

# Pinterest

Learn how to leverage Pinterest in your real estate business.
- 📖 Using Pinterest
- 📖 Creating Your Pinterest Business Page
- 📖 Pinterest Applications

Pinterest is one of the fastest growing social media platforms. According to comScore, Pinterest was the fastest independent site to hit 10 million monthly uniques in the USA. As participation on Pinterest continues to climb, businesses are also quickly discovering ways to connect with individuals. Pinterest is all about visual sharing.

Using Pinterest

Pinterest can be engaging before, during and after a real estate transaction. Let your community know you have you a Business Page and to share photos. Share photos from community events to engage current residents and entice future residents.

So how do you use Pinterest?
1. Think visual.

NOTES

_____

_____

_____

_____

_____

2. Organize your boards - consider your audience
3. Be descriptive so your visitors are compelled to repin
4. Use relevant keywords to be found easily
5. Engage, don't sell

Creating Your Pinterest Business Page

1. Join as a business - http://business.pinterest.com/

NOTE: *unlocking a technology tidbit for you*

Select a username the same as or similar to your other social media platforms to make it easier for people to find you.

2. Complete the information requested and Create Account.

3. Confirm your email address.

4. Your Business Page is created.

5. The next step is to accept some Boards and then you can create your own.

NOTES

_____

_____

_____

_____

_____

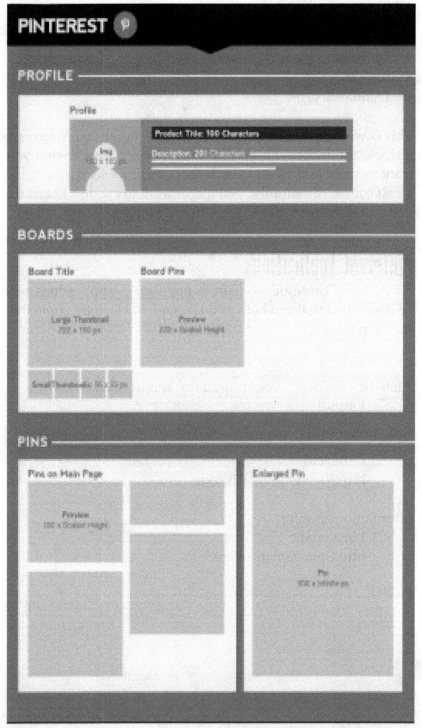

Ways to Organize Your Boards

- Property Boards
- Decorating Ideas
- Neighborhood Boards
- Listings Boards

This is where you can share home decor, home improvement, recipes, and more with your followers. Think about what you want to share and create boards for each of those. If you are in a golf course community, you might want to create a board for golf and share pins there. Be creative and think outside the box.

Pinterest Applications

As Pinterest continues to gain in popularity, applications will be developed that can help you leverage it. Here are some that can help you:

Analytic - measures your popularity and/or reach:
- ☐ Pinpuff
   http://pinpuff.com/pinfluence.php

- ☐ Pinreach
   http://www.pinreach.com/

Information Sharing
- ☐ Pinstamatic
   http://pinstamatic.com/

NOTES

_____

_____

_____

_____

_____

 **Twitter**

Learn how to leverage Twitter in your real estate business.
- 📖 Using Twitter
- 📖 140 Characters
- 📖 Hashtags
- 📖 Twitter Applications

What is Twitter?

Twitter is a microblogging platform that enables you to share information in 140 characters or less. You can attach a link or media, as long as it is part of the 140 characters.

How can I benefit from using Twitter?
1. Learn about your community
2. Listen to what others are saying
3. Listen to what your competitors are saying
4. Engage with businesses in your industry
5. Engage with your community and build a following
6. Ask questions

NOTES

_____

_____

_____

_____

_____

Using Twitter

Twitter presents an opportunity for quick, interactive conversations. A quick explanation of Twitter is: when you search for something on the internet, you can find what exists. But when you search that topic on Twitter, you hear what people are saying about it. As a realtor, you want to be part of the conversation. You also want to monitor what is being said about you, and/or your real estate business. And there are tools that can help you with this. Twitter is available on your desktop, smartphone and tablet.

When you sign up for Twitter, you should input the following information:

Photo: Upload an image that relates to you and/or your profile. Don't leave this blank.

Name: This should be your name, name of your business or related to your business, ie. cobbrealty.

Location: Geo-location is becoming more critical. Note that you can always edit your profile. So if you relocate to another city, add it to your profile, or change your location.

Website: This should be your website or your office website so that people know where to go to learn more about you and/or your business

Bio: Be informative, you only have 160 characters. This should not be a sales pitch.

Facebook: You can elect to post your Tweets to Facebook. Keep in mind that not everyone uses Twitter. So

NOTES

_____

_____

_____

_____

_____

sharing your Tweets on Facebook helps to engage that community as well.

Remember to save changes.

When you first join Twitter, you should explore and listen. Look for influencers to follow. Listen to what they say and share the information by retweeting it. As you become more comfortable, engage in conversations.

Let your website readers know that you are on Twitter. Add a link to your Twitter account on your website. This can be done through a plugin or if you want to use specific icons, you can create a text widget with a hyperlink to your account.

Twitter Symbols

Understanding the *symbol shorthand* of Twitter can help you to be more engaging. The four basics you need to know are:

Reply	Click this option and you will be able to automatically reply to the person who tweeted the original statement
Retweet	Click this option to share something someone else said
DM	DM before a user's name is a direct message - which is private between you and them. You need to be connected in order to DM each other.
Favorite	Sometimes you just want to save a tweet and by clicking Favorite, it will save it

NOTES

_____

_____

_____

_____

_____

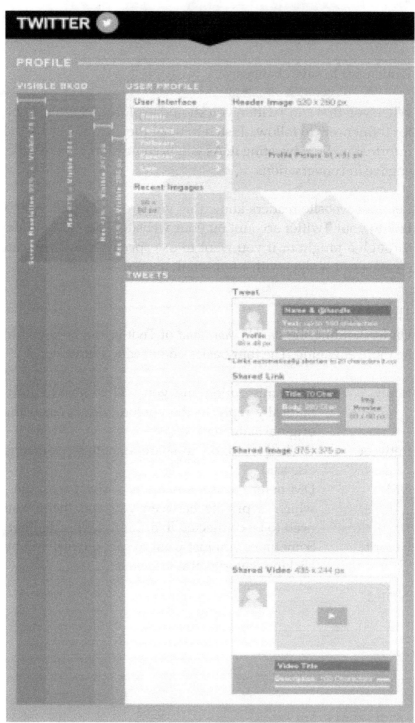

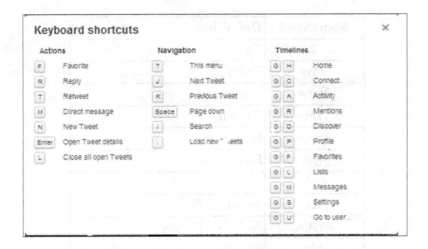

Say it in less than 140

There is a strategy to using Twitter and being able to make statements in less than 140 characters. And I believe that you should use 120 characters, so that you leave enough character space for people to retweet you without editing your statement. Here are some tips on how to make engaging comments on Twitter:

1. Shorthand - using common abbreviations are a great way to shorten your statements. Industry jargon can also be helpful in shortening your Tweets (see some Twitter shorthand on the next pages).

2. Remember grammar. Even though you are trying to keep it short, maintain proper grammar and sentence structure. A missing period or punctuation can change the meaning of your statement.

3. Be engaging. Twitter is all about engagement and learning. Share information, but don't sell. And add humor when-

NOTES

_____

_____

_____

_____

_____

Shorthand	Definition
2	To
2day	Today
2mrw	Tomorrow
2nt	Tonight
4ever	Forever
4gm	Forgive me
4sale	For sale
abt	About
AFAIK	As Far As I Know
b/c	Because
B2B	Business To Business
B2C	Business To Consumer
b4	Before
BBIAB	Be Back In A Bit
BBL	Be Back Later
bf	Boyfriend
BFF	Best Friend Forever
BFN	Bye For Now
bgd	Background
BR	Best Regards
BRB	Be Right Back
chk	Check
cld	Could
clk	Click
cre8	Create
CYE	Check Your Email
deets	Details
DIY	Do It Yourself
DM	Direct Message
EM	Email
EMA	Email Address

Shorthand	Definition
F2F	Face To Face
FAQ	Frequently Asked Questions
fb	Facebook
FF	Follow Friday
FWIW	For What Its Worth
FYI	For Your Information
HT	Heard Through
IC	I See
ICYMI	In Case You Missed It
IDK	I Don't Know
IMO	In My Opinion
IRL	In Real Life
LOL	Laugh Out Loud
NTS	Note To Self
OH	Overheard
PRT	Please Retweet
ROFL	Rolling On The Floor Laughing
SB	Small Business
SM	Social Media
TFTF	Thanks For The Follow
TMB	Tweet Me Back
TMI	Too Much Information
WTV	Whatever
YOYO	You're On Your Own

NOTES

_____

_____

_____

_____

_____

ever possible.

4. Get to the point. You only have 140 characters (or if you want to be retweeted, 120 characters). Say what you need to.

5. DON'T USE ALL CAPS. (how did that feel?) Using all caps makes the reader feel like you are yelling at them, and it's very disengaging. Write your message like you would write a note and stick to the upper/lower case system.

6. Think like your reader. You only have their attention for a brief moment and every word counts. Create interest, show an action.

Hashtags

Hashtags cannot be "owned". So unlike a domain name, you need to select a hashtag that is unique, but easy enough for your community to remember. Before you prepare all of your marketing materials with your hashtag, search it on Twitter to see if it is already being used. Realtors can use hashtags for Tweets referencing a community that they represent. While hashtags are most commonly used for events, realtors can take advantage of this feature to "organize" and manage their Twitter account.

Twitter now offers hashtag buttons to make it easier for you to share this information. Information about these buttons can be found here: https://twitter.com/about/resources/buttons#hashtag. And since Twitter provides you with the HTML code (Preview and Code), you can copy the code provided, paste it into a text widget and quickly add the button to

NOTES

_____

_____

_____

_____

_____

your WordPress site to share the information.

Understanding the Twitter numbers

- Every account can follow 2,000 users total. Once you've followed 2,000 users, there are limits to the number of additional users you can follow. This number is different for each account and is based on your ratio of followers to following; this ratio is not published. Follow limits cannot be lifted by Twitter and everyone is subject to limits, even high profile and API account
- Every Twitter account is technically unable to follow more than 1,000 users per day, in addition to the account-based limits above.
- Each Twitter account can create up to 20 lists
- Each list can include up to 500 users
- You can make your lists public or private
- Followers can add you and/or follow your lists
- There is no limit on how many lists **you** can be on
- There is no limit on how people can follow **you**

You can create your own influencer lists to help you manage your Twitter account. Much like a file folder or address book, name your lists something you will remember, but that somebody else would understand as well. Your list names are public and a reflection of you and your business.

How to create a list:
1. Sign into your Twitter account
2. Click the gear icon on the right hand side of your navigation menu

NOTES

_____

_____

_____

_____

_____

3. Select Lists from the drop down menu
4. Click on Create List
5. Complete the information requested and select whether you want the list to be public or private. Note that your list name can only be 25 characters
6. Search for people you want on the list.
7. Once you find someone, you can click Follow *or* you can click the icon of the man and scroll to select Add or remove from lists ...
8. That's it. You can continue to add people to your list. Once you have created your list, you can add future people you follow by selecting their Twitter name and again click the icon of the man and scroll to select Add or remove from lists... Once you have multiple lists, you will need to select the list you want to add them to.

Twitter Chats

As we discussed on page 22, you can also participate in Twitter chats. Becoming involved in a Twitter Chat also helps you prepare to lead your own chat. As you become more comfortable with a chat, you will become more knowledgeable. You also want to become familiar with tools that can help you participate, and possibly lead, a chat.

- Top social media Twitter chats can be found: http://socialfresh.com/twitter-chats.
- Search this wiki by subject for chat that is relevant to your business: http://www.gnosisarts.com/home/Tweetchat_Wiki/By_Subject

NOTES

_____

_____

_____

_____

Twitter Dashboards

As your Twitter following grows, it will become difficult to read what everyone is saying. And another benefit of lists is that you can create a "list" stream on your dashboard application to keep up to date with their comments. A dashboard application offers you the ability to view several streams of information at one time, and most will offer the ability to include some of your other social media profiles.

Here are two Twitter dashboard applications we use:

☐ Hootsuite
http://hootsuite.com
This dashboard offers the ability to include your LinkedIn, Facebook, Google+, and more. It also offers scheduling of Tweets and analytics. Their premium version offers additional features.

☐ Tweetdeck
http://tweetdeck.com
This dashboard application is primarily for Twitter and also allows you to schedule your Tweets. You can also manage multiple accounts. It also offers notification alerts that will let you know when things are sent to your profile.

Both applications offer mobile and desktop versions.

NOTES

_____

_____

_____

_____

_____

Twitter Applications

There are several applications that will help you manage and grow your Twitter followng. These can be used to find new followers, grow your community, and engage your followers.

Commuity Building

☐ Buffer
http://bufferapp/

☐ InBoxQ
http://www.inboxq.com/

☐ Timely
http://timely.is/

Manage Your Account

☐ Tweepi
http://tweepi.com/

Lists

☐ List.ly
http://list,ly/
Curates your social media

☐ Listorious
http://listorious.com
Twitter lists to help you find someone by topic,
region, or profession, all of the data is compiled
from the tens of thousands of list curators

NOTES

_____

_____

_____

_____

_____

☐ Twitlist
http://www.twitlist.com
The application makes managing lists easy.

☐ Twitlist Manager
http://twitlistmanager.com/
Helps you manage your Twitter lists.

Surveys and Polls

☐ Twtpoll
http://twtpoll.com
Create polls via Twitter to engage your followers
and ask questions

☐ Polleverywhere
http://www.polleverywhere.com
Creative quick polls for research engagement,
and gatherine live responses

Group Management

☐ GroupTweet
http://www.grouptweet.com
Allows multiple users to share one Twitter account
so that your tweets are from your company profile,
but many people can share the responsibility of
updating the company account.

NOTES

_____

_____

_____

_____

_____

Influencers

☐ Followerwonk
http://followerwonk.com
Twitter analytics, follower segmentation, social graph tracking, and more

☐ Topsy
http://topsy.com
Real time insight into conversations

☐ Twellow
http://ww.twellow.com
Offers a directory of public Twitter accounts, with hundreds of categories and search features to help you find people who matter to you including demographics and location

☐ Tweetgrid
http://tweetgrid.com
A Twitter search dashboard that enables you to search up to 9 different topics in realtime. As new tweets are created, they are automatically updated in the grid without you having to refresh the page.

NOTES

_____

_____

_____

_____

_____

 **YouTube**

Learn how to leverage YouTube in your real estate business.
    📖 Creating Your Channel
    📖 Using YouTube

What is YouTube?

YouTube is a video-sharing website on which users can upload, share, and view videos. It is also owned by Google, which as we discussed earlier means that you can add it to your Google+ profile for Google Authorship.

How can I benefit from using YouTube?
1. You can embed informational videos on your website
2. You can link to videos on YouTube
3. You can upload videos to your channel from your phone
4. Engage with businesses in your industry
5. Engage with your community and build a following
6. Share information

NOTES

_____

_____

_____

_____

_____

Using YouTube

Since YouTube is a Google product, you can watch, like and subscribe just by logging into YouTube with your Google account. But to create a channel, there are a few more steps, and you can have a personal channel and business channel which is helpful in keeping your videos separate.

To set up a business account:
1. Sign into YouTube
2. Click on your name on the right hand side of your screen and a select All My Channels from the popup menu.
3. If you want to make a YouTube channel for a Google+ page that you manage, you can choose it here. Otherwise, click Create a new channel and go to Step 6.
4. If you created a Google+ page for your business earlier, you should see it as one of the options. Select that option and click on Create A Channel.
5. You will now see that your Google+ profile and YouTube channel are linked. Click OK.
6. Fill out the details to create your new channel.
7. Add a link to channel on your website.

Now that you have set up your business account, you can create videos and upload them to YouTube. While many real estate professionals may decide to upload property videos, there are other options that can benefit you:
- neighborhood tours
- information helpful to buyers and sellers
- interviews with industry partners on key topics

NOTES

_____

_____

_____

_____

_____

©TentSocial Created by (http://www.tentsocial.com), designed by Curious Ink (http://www.curiousink.ca)

Tips for using videos:

1. Be prepared. Plan your video ahead of time so that you are prepared and focused. As you are starting out, ask family and friends to view the video before you upload it. See if they understand the message, if you were able to get to the point, and if they enjoyed it. Be prepared for feedback.

2. Part of successful preparation is being able to appear real. You do not want to come off scripted. A video is a true reflection of who you are, and you want the best representa-

NOTES

_____

_____

_____

_____

_____

tion possible. If you are taking the video, you are in control.
3. While video is great, you only have people's attention for a short time. So keep your videos between 2 – 5 minutes in length.
4. You don't need expensive equipment, but you do need equipment that offers quality video and good sound.
5. Get started. The only way you will become more comfortable with videos is to produce them. You don't need to upload them to YouTube until you are ready. But once you start, you will become more comfortable and realize the benefits of videos on your website.

As you create videos and upload them to YouTube, you can share them across your social media platforms and on your website. Sharing YouTube videos on your website:
1. Click Share under the video on YouTube
2. Select Embed. You can edit the size of the video by selecting from the drop down on Video Size.
3. Copy the HTML code and paste it into your website.
4. You can modify the privacy settings as you like also.

NOTES

_____

_____

_____

_____

_____

Beyond The Inbox

Learn how to use the power of email
- 📖 Understanding email
- 📖 CAN-SPAM
- 📖 Creating a Campaign
- 📖 Leveraging email subscribers

Email campaigns

Understanding how to leverage an email campaign to engage your readers and increase your reach can be critical to the success of your business. Email offers you the opportunity to share content, area information and social media directly with your reader.

Understanding email

Email marketing is a great way to build a community. One of the benefits of an email is that it is delivered to your readers without them needing to visit your website or navigate for information. You can update them and invite them to visit specific links for more information. And most email marketing appli-

NOTES

_____

_____

_____

_____

_____

cations will share analytics with you including open rates. An open rate is an indication of the number of people who opened or viewed a particular email message.

CAN-SPAM

One of the things you need to understand before developing an email campaign is the CAN-SPAM Act. The acronym stands for Controlling the Assault of Non-Solicited Pornography And Marketing Act of 2003. What does this mean to you? Violating the guidelines of the Act can result in a fine of up to $16,000 per violation, which can be costly. So clearly understanding the guidelines can be critical to your success.

The following page provides the guidelines as per the FTC Guidelines.

1. **Don't use false or misleading header information**. Your "From," "To," "Reply-To," and routing information – including the originating domain name and email address – must be accurate and identify the person or business who initiated the message.

2. **Don't use deceptive subject lines**. The subject line must accurately reflect the content of the message.

3. **Identify the message as an ad**. The law gives you a lot of leeway in how to do this, but you must disclose clearly and conspicuously that your message is an advertisement.

Notes

_____

_____

_____

_____

4. **Tell recipients where you're located**. Your message must include your valid physical postal address. This can be your current street address, a post office box you've registered with the U.S. Postal Service, or a private mailbox you've registered with a commercial mail receiving agency established under Postal Service regulations.

5. **Tell recipients how to opt out of receiving future email from you**. Your message must include a clear and conspicuous explanation of how the recipient can opt out of getting email from you in the future. Craft the notice in a way that's easy for an ordinary person to recognize, read, and understand. Creative use of type size, color, and location can improve clarity. Give a return email address or another easy Internet-based way to allow people to communicate their choice to you. You may create a menu to allow a recipient to opt out of certain types of messages, but you must include the option to stop all commercial messages from you. Make sure your spam filter doesn't block these opt-out requests.

6. **Honor opt-out requests promptly**. Any opt-out mechanism you offer must be able to process opt-out requests for at least 30 days after you send your message. You must honor a recipient's opt-out request within 10 business days. You can't charge a fee, require the recipient to give you any personally identifying information beyond an email address, or make the recipient take any step other than sending a reply email or visit-

NOTES

_____

_____

_____

_____

_____

ing a single page on an Internet website as a condition for honoring an opt-out request. Once people have told you they don't want to receive more messages from you, you can't sell or transfer their email addresses, even in the form of a mailing list. The only exception is that you may transfer the addresses to a company you've hired to help you comply with the CAN-SPAM Act.

7. **Monitor what others are doing on your behalf.** The law makes clear that even if you hire another company to handle your email marketing, you can't contract away your legal responsibility to comply with the law. Both the company whose product is promoted in the message and the company that actually sends the message may be held legally responsible.

For more information and answers to some of your questions, please visit: http://business.ftc.gov/documents/bus61-can-spam-act-compliance-guide-business. Once you have a clear understanding of what is and what is not allowed in email, you can begin to develop your email campaigns.

Creating A Campaign

You can create multiple email campaigns depending on the needs of your business. In addition you can create multiple email lists to strategically leverage your email campaign. As you begin to leverage email for your business, you will understand how to create multiple lists and use them to increase

NOTES

_____

_____

_____

_____

the interaction with your audience. You can offer different information to each of these lists based on how you use them.

The email provider you select may also offer different strategies for your campaigns including RSS, A/B Testing, and more.

So what does this mean:
1. Mailing list 1 may be the subscribers from your website
2. Mailing list 2 may be members of a local organization
3. Mailing list 3 may be former clients

Some things to remember when creating your campaign:
- Did you offer a plain text version that works like your HTML version?
- Do all of the links in your email work and are they going to the right location?
- Are you using <alt tags and are they working properly, i.e, are images visible?
- Do you personalize your emails and if so, are you requiring that information on your subscribe form?
- Are you tracking your links with analytics?
- Are you providing an opt-out on your newsletters?
- Have you tested your email in different inboxes and browsers?
- Are you abiding by your email provider's CAN-SPAM policies?

Leveraging Email Subscribers

As you begin to plan your strategy, you may want to leverage each of these lists in a different manner to market your busi-

NOTES

_____

_____

_____

_____

_____

ness. As you continue to grow your list, you should be strategic in how you organize your subscribers. This can help you in leveraging this segment of your community.

Growing Your List

Understanding how to legitimately grow your list is as important as understanding what you can't do. Here is a list of how to *strategically* grow your list:

- Collect business cards and follow-up with individual one-on-one emails. Introduce yourself and add a reminder of how you met, while providing some content that might be of interest to the recipient that would make them want to subscribe to your newsletter. For example, they can download a whitepaper or ebook relevant to home buying or selling by subscribing to your newsletter.

- You cannot import a list from someone else into your list. So if you would like to market your business to a specific audience, ask someone at that organization to allow you to write some guest content for *their* newsletter and offer the readers a link to subscribe to *your* newsletter to stay current on your news and events.

- If you are an exhibitor at an event and offer attendees an opportunity to subscribe to your email list, create a "group" off of your main mailing list that describes who these subscribers are. This way you can send

NOTES

_____

_____

_____

_____

_____

specific communication to them as well as your general newsletter, offering an opportunity to reacquaint yourself with them and eliminate being tagged as spam.

There are several situations that can cause your email account to be "blacklisted" by your provider. And while different email providers may have different standards, you should realize that the final decision maker is your reader. If they feel your email is being sent erroneously and mark it as SPAM, you have lost a potential member of your community, and possibly a client. So while you may a large email list, it is more important to have an engaged community.

Email Providers

There are several email providers, including individuals and small agencies that can help you with your email campaigns. Here is a sampling:

- ☐ AWeber
  http://www.aweber.com/

- ☐ Constant Contact
  http://www.constantcontact.com

- ☐ MailChimp
  http://mailchimp.com/

- ☐ Silverpop
  http://www.silverpop.com/

NOTES

_____

_____

_____

_____

_____

NOTES

_____

_____

_____

_____

_____

 # QR Codes

Learn what QR Codes are and how to use them; and how RFID technology is also becoming a game changer

- 📖 Benefits of QR Code technology
- 📖 How to use QR Code
- 📖 What is RFID and how do I use it

QR Code Technology

Quick response technology, better known as QR Codes, were first designed for the automobile industry. Their popularity has now grown beyond the automotive industry due to the fast readability and large storage capacity compared to standard UPC barcodes.

Benefits of QR Code Technology

As smartphone use continues to grow, quick acquisition of information becomes more of a priority. The ability to quickly scan information can aid in customer engagement.

NOTES

_____

_____

_____

_____

_____

Using QR Codes

QR Codes make it easy to share information.

- Print postcards and flyers with QR codes that redirect to a web page that you can update with information on a listing. Even though the QR Code is to a specific page, the page does not have to be static.
- A QR Code can lead to an opt-in for information updates
- Create a contest with a call to action. As readers scan the QR Code, they can be entered to win a prize related to your promotion
- Use free QR services like bit.ly that offer short URLs and tracking.
- Create an event using QR Codes like an Open House Caravan

NOTE: *unlocking a technology tidbit for you*

For a directory of QR Code resources, visit http://qrmediaguide.com or http://qrmedia.us

While there are several different resources available to create QR codes, here are some that are relatively easy to use. You will need a QR Code creator/generator and a QR Code reader to execute a campaign.

NOTES

_____

_____

_____

_____

_____

QR Code Generators

In order to use QR Codes, you will need to create them. This is done through QR Code Generators. There are several websites that offer this service, and we will review a few here.

☐ Bit.ly
http://bit.ly

The QR Code Generator also offers analytics on their QR Codes which would be helpful to determine ROI. Since QR Codes may not be familiar to your attendees, you could also test adoption of this technology prior to your event, to ensure that your attendees are aware of it and understand how to use it. The analytics will help you see the results.

1. Click on Stats on top nav bar
2. Select your link from the list that appears and click on it
3. Click on the QR Code next to the shortened URL link and it will open in a new window. Right click on the QR Code to Save Image As, and save as a .jpeg file to use in your QR Code campaign.

NOTE: *unlocking a technology tidbit for you*

Always test your QR Codes before you use to make sure that when scanned, the result is what you want.

NOTES

_____

_____

_____

_____

_____

Some other QR Code Generators:

☐ **Delivr**
http://delivr.com/qr-code-generator

☐ **BeQRious**
http://beqrious.com/qr-code-generator/

QR Code Reader

While you may hear some people say "just scan it with your camera", all this will produce is a picture. To scan a QR code, you need a QR Code Reader that understands how to process the code to offer you the message/destination intended. So here are some readers that you can download and use on your smartphone or tablet:

☐ i-Nigma
http://www.i-nigma.com

☐ NeoReader
http://get.neoreader.com/

☐ Norton Labs Snap
http://labs.norton.com/

QR Code Campaigns

This techology has had some barriers to adoption, but offers a tremendous amount of participation. It also provides a fun and mysterious factor by not knowing what the scanned result will be.

NOTES

_____

_____

_____

_____

_____

NOTE: *unlocking a technology tidbit for you*

Remember the people without smartphones. Provide a link to the landing page that the QR code is sending people to, so that everyone is included.

☐ The World Park
http://www.theworldpark.com/campaign/
A QR Code Campaign enabled the NY Central Park Tourism the opportunity to re-engage visitors by creating an outdoor mobile museum. The Campaign turned Central Park into an interactive board game.

☐ Heineken UCode
http://www.youtube.com/watch?v=0RrXcm89FAo
Heineken offered attendees at a music festival the opportunity to share personal information that was printed out as a QR Code sticker and could be scanned. The QR Codes became icebreakers, increased attendee participation and also created some new friendships. Heineken saw a 200% increase over planned participation.

Each of these campaigns had one thing in common: engaging viewers without selling anything. They increased brand awareness and participation. The creative use of technology was strategic and economical.

NOTES

_____

_____

_____

_____

_____

Include suggestions for QR code Readers in your QR Code campaign to help expedite user participation.

NOTE: *unlocking a technology tidbit for you*

What is RFID and how do I use it?

Much like QR Codes, RFID is new technology and adoption can be slow. But making usage fun and inclusive can help with that as well as making your event more interactive. RFID stands radio-frequency identification. NFC is near-field communication technology, and is wireless and uses radio-frequency electromagnetic fields to transfer data. NFC enables two-way communication at a very close distance. Much like a QR Code, a tag can store small amounts of data that can then be transferred to other devices wirelessly.

NFC Tags

☐ Tagstand
http://www.tagstand.com/

☐ Access Pass
http://www.accesspasses.com

NOTES

_____

_____

_____

_____

_____

Mobile Apps for Realtors

Learn how to use the power of mobile apps
- 📖 What is a native app
- 📖 Leveraging mobile apps for your business

Understanding mobile technology

Understanding the technologies that are available and what they offer will help you decide which ones to use and how to integrate them into your business, for yourself and your customers.

NOTE: *unlocking a technology tidbit for you*

While an app might be nice for a realtor, a responsive website is a more realistic and economical option for independent realtors.

NOTES

_____

_____

_____

_____

_____

What is a native app

One of the most common distinctions between a web app and a native app is that a native app does not require internet access. For meeting attendees this can be critical, especially at convention centers where wifi connectivity can be sporadic. However, there is a benefit to offering both. That would be to ensure access to information for customers without smartphones. Consider your entire community when using any technology.

Benefits of a native app

- **Native apps are responsive and functional**. This makes them quicker to respond to user requests.
- **Cellular coverage.** Web-based applications, by definition, require web access which may not always be available. Native apps can function without cellular coverage.

Benefits of an HTML5 app

There has been confusion between web apps and HTML 5 apps. To clarify, an HTML5 app is in fact a web app. However, every web app is not HTML5. The term "Web App" is used to identify any application that needs some form of a webserver to run.

Pros: Develop once for all platforms
Updates on server

Cons: Internet connection is required
Accessible through browser, not downloaded from app store
Current access to GPS and camera is limited

NOTES

_____

_____

_____

_____

_____

Here are some real estate application platforms:
N - native   H - HTML5   M - mobile

- ☐ The App Builder
  http://www.theappbuilder.com
  H, N

- ☐ Smarter Agent
  http://home.smarteragent.com/
  M

- ☐ My Pocket Property
  http://mypocketproperty.com/
  M, N

- ☐ Realty Agency App
  http://www.realtyagentapp.com/
  iPad

Using that Smartphone

A smartphone or tablet offers realtors the ability to have access to a significant amount of information from the "field". This provides increased productivity and potential sales. Several apps are available only for the Android while others may only be available on the iPhone/iPad. Other applications are available on both platforms.

There are several websites that offer the MLS listings and are available to the general public as well as agents. These include:

NOTES

_____

_____

_____

_____

_____

☐ Homes.com
http://www.homes.com/mobile-apps/

☐ HotPads
http://hotpads.com/

☐ IDXBroker
http://www.idxbroker.com/

☐ Realtor.com
http://www.realtor.com/mobile

☐ Trulia
http://www.trulia.com/mobile/iphoneagent/

☐ Zillow
http://www.zillow.com/mobile/

NOTES

_____

_____

_____

_____

_____

Creating your own app

As the use of smartphones and tablets increases, so will the need for a mobile app for your business. And with that, comes the ability to create your own app. The App Builder offers you the ability to create an app for your business, but also to build general information and pages to help you engage your users.

☐ THE APP BUILDER
http://www.theappbuilder.com

Some other websites that can help you with your own app include:

☐ Smarter Agent
http://home.smarteragent.com/

☐ My Pocket Property
http://mypocketproperty.com/

☐ Realty Agency App
http://www.realtyagentapp.com/iPAD

NOTES

_____

_____

_____

_____

_____

☐ MindSea
http://mindsea.com/

☐ Pensacola Apps
http://pensacolarealestateapp.com/

NOTE: *unlocking a technology tidbit for you*

While a mobile app might be a "nice to have", a well thought out responsive website will provide all of the same features, without you having to maintain the website and the application.

NOTES

_____

_____

_____

_____

_____

Real Estate Detail

Features to include in a mobile app:
- Property search by city, state or ZIP-code, that is also GPS enabled and options for display of results
- Frequent MLS (multiple listing system) information updates;
- Advanced functionality with additional search filters, such as proximity, price range, number of bedrooms and baths, garages, pools, other interior and exterior features;
- QR codes scanner linking directly to property listing;
- Google mapping with Street View and driving directions;
- Details of the real estate (photos, price, square footage, room dimensions, contact person details, etc.);
- Neighborhood information (schools, stores, etc.);
- Advice and testimonials;
- Price comparisons;
- Social media sharing and links

NOTES

_____

_____

_____

_____

_____

NOTES

_____

_____

_____

_____

_____

Location Based Apps

Learn how to leverage your location
- 📖 What is location based technology
- 📖 Using location based apps

Navigating location based technology

Understanding location based technologies that are available and what they offer will help you decide which ones to use and how to integrate them into your real estate business.

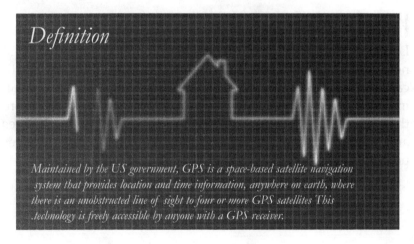

Definition

Maintained by the US government, GPS is a space-based satellite navigation system that provides location and time information, anywhere on earth, where there is an unobstructed line of sight to four or more GPS satellites This technology is freely accessible by anyone with a GPS receiver.

NOTES

_____

_____

_____

_____

_____

What is location based technology

Location based apps (LBS) utilize GPS (Global Positioning System) information. This technology has come together to offer location-based social networking. Leveraging this technology can help to grow your community. Location based technology can be used to:

- requesting the nearest business or service, such as an ATM or restaurant
- turn by turn navigation to any address
- locating people on a map displayed on the mobile phone
- location-based mobile advertising
- recommend social events in a city
- connecting with other people nearby games where your location is part of the game play, for example your movements during your day make your avatar move in the game or your position unlocks content.

Using Location Based Apps

Location based apps help to engage your followers in social networking and can help to grow your community. One application, Poynt, states "the free personal concierge that turns you into a local expert, wherever you are." Foursquare offers more than "check-ins", it offers a game component including badges and mayorships; while also offering information on services near your location.

NOTES

_____

_____

_____

_____

_____

☐ Foursquare
https://foursquare.com

Foursquare offers free services to businesses including claiming their venue and offering specials. As a realtor, you can create a "venue" for your office. You can leverage Foursquare by offering specials to visitors. And once you claim your venue, you will also have access to analytics including:

- Total daily check-ins over time
- Your most recent visitors
- Your most frequent visitors
- Gender breakdown of your customers
- What time of day people check in
- Portion of your venue's foursquare check-ins that are broadcast to Twitter and Facebook

As visitors check-in to your venue, they may also be provided with some suggestions nearby. For out-of-town visitors, this can be a great way to connect.

Foursquare Specials Nearby:

F1	FL
Receive 25% off any hair services	Receive a COMPLIMENTARY Draft Beer or glass of House Wine with Purchase of any entree when you

NOTES

_____

_____

_____

_____

_____

This data can be helpful in planning future marketing programs. Looking at the analytics also helps you see the use of the application and integration with other social media platforms like Twitter and Facebook.

Other "check-in" apps are available, but offer limited services compared to Foursquare. However, if these applications are used by your community, then you should investigate them.

NOTES

_____

_____

_____

_____

_____

Location based apps are an evolving technology and applications like Foursquare are surviving by understanding how people are using it and offering services to respond to this. Other applications are coming into play and as usage increases, it will become clearer how LBS is evolving and responding to different types of content generation and aggregation. The analytics being offered by Foursquare provides a window into this by leverage the data to understand consumer behavior.

Location based apps for Realtors

The following are apps that can be helpful for realtors and are available on iPhone and Android.

☐ Guidebook
http://guidebook.com

☐ AroundMe
http://www.aroundme.com

☐ Poynt
http://www.poynt.com

☐ Yelp
http://www.yelp.com/yelpmobile

NOTES

_____

_____

_____

_____

_____

NOTES

_____

_____

_____

_____

_____

The Brand You Policy

Learn what policies and procedures you should have in place:
- 📖 Social Media Implications: Risks & Rewards
- 📖 Your website/company privacy policy
- 📖 Your company Social Media policy
- 📖 Your customer service policy

Social Media: Risks and Rewards

As social media has become a pervasive and omnipresent means for commercial communication, it is imperative that users of social media understand the impact social media has on the protection and exploitation of intellectual property.

> ❝ He said, she said, they said, we said. As long as they acted responsibly and showed respect, and the customer is engaged, we're OK. Right?

NOTES

_____

_____

_____

_____

_____

What is your intellectual property?

According to the US Patent & Trademark Office, intellectual property is:

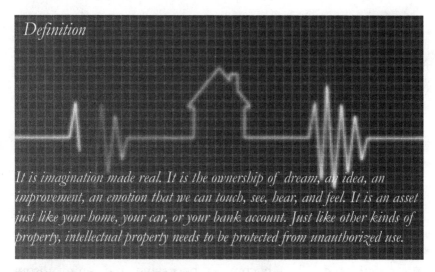

Definition

It is imagination made real. It is the ownership of dream, an idea, an improvement, an emotion that we can touch, see, hear, and feel. It is an asset just like your home, your car, or your bank account. Just like other kinds of property, intellectual property needs to be protected from unauthorized use.

Naming your business and/or domain name

There are several factors that impact the ownership of your domain name. If you know that or think that there is an issue with your business name, it is best to consult a professional to pursue the situation. If you own a trademark or service mark (whether federally registered or not), you should be diligent about preventing any trademark infringement, which would include someone else using your domain name. ICANN's Uniform Domain Name Dispute Resolution Policy requires that each of the following exist in order to pursue a dispute:

(i) your domain name is identical or confusingly similar to

NOTES

_____

_____

_____

_____

_____

a trademark or service mark in which the complainant has rights; and

(ii) you have no rights or legitimate interests in respect of the domain name; and

(iii) your domain name has been registered and is being used in bad faith.

You should also ensure that when you purchase a domain name, that you are the owner of the domain. Ownership of a domain can be verified through a WhoIs search at http://whois.com.

As you perform your domain name search, ensure that the domains you select are not trademarked. Just because a domain name is available, does not mean it is not trademarked.

Once you have your domain, you should prepare a privacy policy for your website, and if applicable, a Terms & Conditions policy. Below are some websites that provide a free privacy policy template that you can use. Depending on the complexity of your privacy policy, you may want to seek the help of a professional.

- ☐ Free Privacy Policy
  http://www.freeprivacypolicy.com/

- ☐ Generate Privacy Policy
  http://www.generateprivacypolicy.com/

NOTES

_____

_____

_____

_____

_____

Real Estate Detail

If you are an independent agent working with other agents/brokers, you should verify if they have a domain name policy and/or any trademark infringement issues.

Social Media Policy

The time has come. Over 1 billion people are using social media and whether you like it or not, they may be talking about you. As you begin to grow your business, you want the best online reputation possible. You might be looking for investors and if they are interested, they will probably research you on the web. You may be collaborating on a Twitter account with co-founders, or sharing admin rights on a Facebook page. Whatever the reason, and whatever the size of your business, having a social media policy in place is just good business.

There are social media policies available on the internet, and much like any other legal document, you may want to review this with a professional. That said, here are some basic things to consider when instituting a social media policy:

NOTES

_____

_____

_____

_____

- Who is in charge of the social media accounts
- Who can give access to use the social media accounts
- Are officers/employees allowed to use their personal accounts to comment on business issues
- How do you want posts credited - i.e., determine if all tweets, posts, etc., should have some "code" in them like a person's initials at the end - this will help to identify who said something
- Ethical standards you want enforced
- Should disclaimers be used when posting
- Specific issues relating to your business that must be included in a social policy

Just like any other HR policy, your Social Media Policy should be updated annually with all employees signing an acknowledgement. As new employees are brought in, they should sign off on the Social Media Policy as well. Here are some websites that can help you create a Social Media Policy:

☐ Policy Tool
http://socialmedia.policytool.net/

☐ Social Policy Generator
http://socialpolicygenerator.com/

Customer Service Policy

There are several considerations in how you manage customer service. And together with your website and social media pol-

NOTES

_____

_____

_____

_____

_____

icy, customer service needs to be incorporated into your company policies and procedures. You should never assume that your employees are clear on what the company expectations are.

Some questions you should consider when creating a customer service policy:
1. When is customer service available? Is this posted in your social media?
2. Are you prepared to offer customer service online?
3. How will you offer customer service online?
4. What are your traditional customer service policies and how will they be adapted to your online environment?

The list could go on, but basically you need to set the ground rules. Even major corporations had to feel their way through this process. A recent blog post from Altimeter Group speaks to Social Media Crisis Prevention. [http://www.altimetergroup.com/2012/10/social-media-crisis-prevention-can-you-defuse-an-f-bomb.html]

As you begin to develop your own policies, you can keep a log on what you see from other companies. Listen to what others are saying. Are some companies more responsive than others? How are they doing it? Make note of what you like, but also what you don't like. These notes can quickly form the outline for your own social media policy.

NOTES

_____

_____

_____

_____

_____

Online Reputation Management

Learn how to:
- 📖 Monitor your online reputation
- 📖 Manage your online reputation

Monitoring your online reputation

We are creatures of habit and tend to not worry about anything until it becomes a problem. Social media enables anyone to say anything. Filters aren't always required, and barometers of truth and integrity don't reside in obvious arenas. That said, we need to monitor what is being said. Review sites enable customers to comment on your services without your consent, and don't always allow you to respond.

And as you have learned in other chapters of this book, frequent updates are received quickly by search engines. It is quite possible for your business to appear in a negative review before your website appears on a search result.

NOTES

_____

_____

_____

_____

_____

You can use several tools to monitor your online reputation. These tools offer an opportunity to automate the monitoring process so that you receive alerts whenever anything is said and can be proactive in remedying the situation. Some of these tools are relevant to your personal online reputation while others include your business reputation.

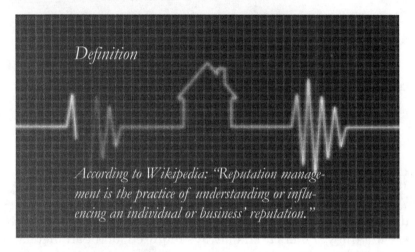

Definition

According to Wikipedia: "Reputation management is the practice of understanding or influencing an individual or business' reputation."

☐ Me on the Web
http://google.com/
Google offers a tool within the Google Dashboard, which can help you understand and manage what people see when they search for you on Google. You can choose to be notified when your personal data appears on the web and also get tips on removing content from Google's search results.

NOTES

_____

_____

_____

_____

_____

◻ Naymz
http://www.naymz.com/
Naymz offers online brand management and calculates your influence across LinkedIn, Facebook, and Twitter. It also offers rewards for members with strong reputation scores.

◻ Reputation
http://www.reputation.com/
This website offers personal and business monitoring through a dashboard that quickly offers you insight into your online reputation. While their personal monitoring is free, their other services are not.

Manage your online reputation

Own your online real estate ... Much like your personal reputation, you want to ensure the integrity of your business. You want to ensure that you "own" your online identify. Think about your business name.

Scenario: You came up with a great name for your business and the .com domain wasn't available. So you went ahead and purchased the .net domain. After your business launched, the .com website went viral and monopolized the internet - only problem is they are an unethical company located in the same state. And now you are suffering

NOTES

_____

_____

_____

_____

_____

the negative impact. Oops!

Scenario: All of your social media efforts have paid off and you are now regarded as a subject matter expert on Twitter. The problem is your Twitter profile name isn't your real name and you never updated your profile to reflect the "real" you. And your other social media platform names are different as well.

As you begin the adventure, consider the journey. What do you want to achieve? Who do you want to be? We mentioned earlier in the book to be consistent in your online presence, and suggested you use Namechk to find out if your "name" is available on the platforms you want. You should also register your name on platforms you aren't currently active on, but may be in the future. As you continue to build your online brand reputation, you want to protect it.

Follow the rules

The ability to place an online review has become a hot button. A medical company paid a fine to the State of New York for placing fake positive reviews on the internet.

As you are trying to remedy a problem, you can sometimes create an even bigger one. The medical company mentioned above, now has several articles about their false reviews on the internet. And companies that have abused review policies can also easily be found on the internet. Their website content over

NOTES

_____

_____

_____

_____

_____

the last few years would probably have moved the negative reviews far down in the search results, but instead they are still suffering the consequences of their unethical actions.

Find out how to remedy a bad review and do it ethically. Google offers tips on handling negative information. Many review sites offer you the ability to respond to negative reviews. While it's never nice to hear something negative, it does present an opportunity to improve your services and learn something. A positive response from you to the negative review offers others an opportunity to see that you are open to improving your business and learning from your community to offer them something better.

Remedy the situation

You can score points in the way you manage negative feedback. And just like developing your online presence, it begins with listening.

1. **LISTEN** - listen to what the reviewer has said. Hear what they are saying.

2. **COMPASSION** - understand what they are saying and why they are saying it. Also consider the situation and develop a plan to action for resolution and reward.

3. **RESOLVE** - reach out to the reviewer to discuss the review and determine how to resolve the problem. Don't disregard their review, it is a learning experience both in what happened, but also how to handle this type of situation.

NOTES

_____

_____

_____

_____

_____

4. **REWARD** - the reviewer offered you an opportunity to improve your business and services. Offer them a reward. This does not have to be monetary, it can be a "thank you", and you hopefully considered and planned for this in step 2.

5. **REVIEW** - how did the situation occur? What could have been done differently to prevent this? Institute any new policies and procedures necessary to prevent it from happening again.

6. **SHARE** - be transparent. Share what you can about the situation through your blog and on social media to present a positive spin on the situation. This should also be done in a timely manner to present your business in a positive manner.

Real Estate Detail

Create an online reputation management policy for your business and keep it updated, Also ensure that you have a Privacy Policy for your website. Protect account access and passwords, including changing passwords regularly and immediately deleting passwords and account access for employees that leave or are dismissed.

NOTES

_____

_____

_____

_____

_____

 # Real Estate Productivity

Learn what tools you can use to increase your productivity:
- 📖 Office Environment
- 📖 Financial Organization
- 📖 Document Management
- 📖 Real Estate Productivity
- 📖 Networking

Office Environment

It is very easy to get lost on the internet and forget about the basics of your business. But setting up and organizing your business is just as important. Your office environment needs to be a comfortable workspace for you. So think about the issues that can affect your workflow:

1. Layout of the room
2. Workspace on your desk
3. Color and lighting of the room
4. Storage
5. Accessibility for meeting client
6. Sound for telephone/conference calls

NOTES

_____

_____

_____

_____

_____

The apps listed are coded - PC (available on desktop/laptop); M (available on mobile); A (Apple store download); G (Google store download)

Financial Organization

There are several online applications to help you with your financial organization. In addition, several banks now offer online deposits in addition to online bill pay.

As a realtor, you probably need to look for financial tools that can help you manage: Basic Accounting, Commission Income, Real Estate Fees and Dues Expenses, Real Estate Education Expense, Office Expenses, Marketing and Advertising, and Vehicle Mileage

NOTES

_____

_____

_____

_____

_____

☐ Free Agent
http://www.freeagent.com/
An online accounting program offering Invoicing, Expense Tracking, UsersTime Tracking, Clients, Account Reports, Project, Data Back-up, Estimates, SSL Security
PC, A (Mobile Agent)

☐ KashFlow
http://www.kashflow.com/
Accounting program that integrates with several other programs including Dropbox, Basecamp, MailChimp, PayPal.
PC, A

☐ Outright
http://outright.com/
This app offers online management of all of your finances including mileage document and tax tracking and reporting.
PC, A

☐ Wave Accounting
https://www.waveapps.com/
A free online accounting program offering invoicing, payroll and accounting options.
PC, A (tablet)

☐ Xero
http://www.xero.com/
An accounting program offering financial report-

NOTES

_____

_____

_____

_____

_____

ing, payroll, expense reports, bill payment, fixed asset depreciation, and integration with several other applications.
PC, A, G

Expense Management

I highlighted the major categories of expenses that you might need as a Real Estate Professional on page 147. Keep these categories in mind as you explore different expense management applications. And since you are probably a "road warrior", you should look for applications that enable you to track expenses from your smartphone and upload expense reports as well as share data with your accounting program.

☐ Expensify
https://www.expensify.com/
This app offers automatic receipt scanning to enable you to go paperless, link your credit cards to receive eReceipts, offers mileage tracking and expense report functionality.
PC, A, G

☐ Expense Cloud
https://www.expensecloud.com/
Offers mobile receipt capture. Add expenses, edit imported credit card data, create, submit and approve expense reports.
PC, A, G

NOTES

_____

_____

_____

_____

_____

Document Management

As a realtor, you handle several documents from listing agreements to sales contracts. Many of these require signatures which can be time consuming, especially during timely transactions. But your smartphone can provide you with quick turnaround as well as file storage of documents.

E-Signature

☐ DocuSign
http://www.docusign.com/
This app enables you to send, sign and save documents on any device.
PC, A, G

☐ Sign My Pad
http://www.autriv.com/products/sign-my-pad/
Enables you to load pdf files to your smartphone and have them signed and sent.
A, G

☐ SignNow
https://signnow.com/
Signing with SignNow enables you to organize, track, and save your documents securely in your account.
PC, A, G

NOTES

_____

_____

_____

_____

_____

☐ TouchSign
http://www.zipform.com/touchsign/
TouchSign included with zipForm® Mobile Web
Edition, allows users to sign their transactions on a
touchscreen tablet.
A, G

Closing Document Management

☐ DotLoop
https://www.dotloop.com/
Enables closing documents to be viewed and
complete the transaction process from offer to
close, online. While the application may be accessible from a smartphone, the company does
not currently appear to offer a native app.
PC

☐ SureClose
http://portal.propertyinfo.com/sureclose
You can post documents to SureClose through
browsing, print-to-file, email or SureScan scanning
solution. Another feature is the ability to reduce
liability and monitor for compliance with a transaction audit trail.
PC, A, G

NOTES

_____

_____

_____

_____

_____

Real Estate Documents

☐ Cartavi
http://cartavi.com/
This app offers the ability to keep all your docs at your fingertips. Store, access and share your transaction documents from wherever you are.
PC, A, G

☐ DocBox2Go
http://www.instanetsolutions.com/docbox.htm
Similar to other document storage applications, but all communications sent through DocBox can include your own branded communications, like your logo, contact information and photo. DocBox2Go requires a DocBox account.
PC, A, G

☐ ZipForm Mobile
http://www.zipform.com/zfmobile
Get property information, seller and buyer information, and list and offer dates along with listing price and deposit. You can quickly list the forms within a transaction, add a new form to a transaction and fill in all of the information for a transaction with the 'Edit' feature. NOTE: Requires zipForm 6 Professional.
PC, A, G

NOTES

_____

_____

_____

_____

_____

Document Storage and Collaboration

☐ Box
https://www.box.com/
You can access, share and collaborate on files anywhere through our award-winning mobile apps. Share folders in a tap, exchange feedback or save files for offline access.
PC, A, G

☐ Dropbox
https://www.dropbox.com/
Dropbox shared folders let you collaborate on specific files. When someone joins a shared folder, the folder appears inside their Dropbox and syncs to their computers automatically.
PC, A, G

☐ Evernote
http://evernote.com/premium/
Evernote Premium offers you bigger upload capacity, access to note history, PDF searching and faster image recognition
PC, A, G

Open Houses

☐ Open House Manager
https://itunes.apple.com/open-house-manager/
A

NOTES

_____

_____

_____

_____

_____

☐ Open Home Pro
http://www.openhomepro.com/iphone
A

Measuring and Floorplans

☐ Magic Plan
http://www.sensopia.com/
Measures and draws our floorplan on the iPad and
iPhone
A

☐ D Photo Measures
http://www.d-solutions.be/d-measures
A picture is worth a thousand words! This powerfull
application let's you draw measures and dimensions on a photo. After photos are marked up with
measurements, they can be send to anyone, or
exported to the media gallery.
G

☐ My Measures
http://www.sis.si/my-measures/
Storing and sharing object dimensions including
rooms, windows, appliances, and more.
A, G

NOTES

_____

_____

_____

_____

_____

Security

☐ Agents Armor
http://agentsarmor.com/
This app offers features that are specific to the
activities that a real estate professional engages in
every day.
A, G

☐ Agent Alarm
http://agentalarm.com/
Set a safety check before you walk into an unfa-
miliar situation and Agent Alarm will actively monitor your safety by checking-in with you on time
intervals that you set.
A, G

☐ SnapSecure
http://www.snapone.com/our-products
This app offers a way to alert others that you're in
danger via a call, email, SMS, or Twitter along with
your GPS location.
PC, A, G

☐ Guardly
https://www.guardly.com
This app offers a variety of security options to connect to authorities, family and friends when you
need help.
A, G

NOTES

_____

_____

_____

_____

_____

☐ Glympse
http://www.glympse.com/
This app allows GPS-enabled mobile phone users to share their location via a Web-based map for a pre-set period of time with anyone they choose. With Glympse, you are in complete control – you choose WHO you want to see your location, WHEN and for HOW LONG.
A, G, B, W

☐ Real Alert
http://www.realalertapp.com/
This app helps you to stay alert and aware of your surroungs and provides quick access to emergency services.
A, G

Real Estate Investment

☐ Property Tracker
http://www.propertytracker.com/
Enables you to analyze potential investment properties from iPhone, and email a professional, branded PDF performance projection to your clients, lenders, and investment partners.
A

☐ Property Evaluator
http://www.realestatetools.com/propertyevaluator/
This application enables you to analyze proper-

NOTES

_____

_____

_____

_____

_____

ties, view a 30 year buy and hold projection, email a professional PDF report to your clients that is branded with your name and logo
A

☐ Property Fixer
http://www.realestatetools.com/propertyfixer/
Property Fixer is designed for real estate investors who are flipping properties
A

☐ Homesnap
http://www.homesnap.com/
Snap a photo of any home to find out all about it. Homesnap draws on our massive homes database to show you how much the home is worth, when it last sold, interior features details, local school ratings, similar listings, nearby sales and more.
A, G

Property Management

☐ The Landlord App
http://www.thelandlordapp.com/
Track rent payments, expenses, Maintain Tenant, Lease and Mortgage Information and more.
A, G

NOTES

_____

_____

_____

_____

_____

Homeowner & Neighborhood Information

☐ HomeZada
http://www.homezada.com/
A home inventory and home improvement app that can be offered to clients to manage their new homes
PC, A, G

☐ Suburb Scout
http://www.915software.com/suburbscout.html-
Suburb Scout can use your current location to search for possible nuisances in your neigborhood including Airports, Landfills, Power Plants, Prisons and Sewage Plants.
A, G

Business of Real Estate

☐ Real Estate Book of Business
http://bookofbusinessapp.com
Allows Brokers to manage "everything" in one place
PC

NOTES

_____

_____

_____

_____

_____

Real Estate CRM

☐ PropertyBase
http://www.propertybase.com/
Working with Salesforce, Propertybase offers CRM
solutions specific to real estate
both residential and commercial.
PC, A, G

☐ Campaigner CRM
http://www.campaignercrm.com/
This CRM unites CRM and email to offer a power-
ful, easy to use tool for your sales team.
PC A, G

☐ Top Producer CRM
http://www.topproducer.com/
Build referrals and build your business with real
estate's most intuitive real estate customer contact management (CRM) software for agents and
brokers
PC, A, G

☐ Trbus CRM
http://www.tribusgroup.com/real-estate-crm-
agents-brokerages/#
This CRM was created by Realtors for Realtors
keeping in mind what you need to be more successful.
PC

NOTES

_____

_____

_____

_____

_____

CMA

☐ Tookit CMA
http://www.realtytools.com/
Comparative Market Analysis reports offers branded presentations
PC, A

☐ Cloud CMA
http://cloudcma.com/agents
Offers branded CMA reports with Dashboard over-
view
PC, A

Customer Feedback

☐ Real Satisfied
http://www.realsatisfied.com/
Send surveys to customers and receive their feedback. This app also offers a WordPress plugin that
can be used on a sidebar.
PC

☐ Homelight
http://www.homelight.com/
Analyzing actual sales data and client reviews to
find agents whose skills match your needs.
PC

NOTES

_____

_____

_____

_____

_____

Marketing

☐ Paperless Post
http://www.paperlesspost.com/
Sending the web's most beautiful
invitations and cards is easy and free.
A

Photographs

☐ 360 Panorama
http://occipital.com/360/app
Capture panoramic views and send instantly to
email, Facebook, Twitter.
A, G, B

Key Control

☐ eKey
http://www.supraekey.com/Products/Pages/eKEY.
aspx
Use your smartphone or tablet as your lockbox
key.
A, B, G

NOTES

_____

_____

_____

_____

_____

Appendix

The following pages offer you keyboard shortcuts and tips for using the platforms discussed in this book.

- Facebook
- Google+
- LinkedIn
- Pinterest
- Twitter
- YouTube

Facebook Keyboard Shortcuts

Facebook keyboard shortcuts vary depending on your technology and browser. If you are using a Windows PC, you will need to use the following keystrokes *before* the number(s) listed below.

WINDOWS
Firefox: Shift + Alt + #
Chrome: Alt + #

If you are using an Apple computer, you will need to use the following keystrokes before the number(s) listed below.

APPLE
Firefox : Control + #
Chrome: Control + Option + #
Safari: Control + Option + #

KEYBOARD SHORTCUTS
1   home
2   timeline/profile
3   friends
4   messages
5   notifications
6   your account settings
7   your privacy settings
8   Facebook's page
9   legal terms
0   help center
l   like/unlike photos
m   new message
?   search

Left and right arrow keys: Skip back and forth between photos

Twitter Keyboard Shortcuts

Unlike Facebook, the Twitter keyboard shortcuts are not browser specific. So you use the same keystrokes regardless of the platform and browser you are using.

NAVIGATION

Shift + Space	Moves the page up
Space	Move the page down
Enter	Closes a specific Tweet
J	Moves to the next Tweet
K	Moves to the previous Tweet
.	Refresh the page
/	Search
?	Menu

TWEET SHORTCUTS

F	Favorite a Tweet
L	Close all open Tweets
M	Direct Message
N	New Tweet
R	Reply
T	Retweet
Enter	Open Tweet details
Escape	Cancel any window

TIMELINE NAVIGATION

All timeline shortcuts are prefixed with a 'G'

G and A	Activity
G and C	Connect
G and D	Discover
G and F	Favorites
G and H	Home
G and L	Lists
G and M	Messages
G and P	Profile
G and R	Mentions
G and S	Settings
G and U	Go to user ...

Keyboard shortcuts

×

Actions

F	Favorite
R	Reply
T	Retweet
M	Direct message
N	New Tweet
Enter	Open Tweet details
L	Close all open Tweets

Navigation

?	This menu
J	Next Tweet
K	Previous Tweet
Space	Page down
/	Search
.	Load new Tweets

Timelines

G H	Home
G C	Connect
G A	Activity
G R	Mentions
G D	Discover
G P	Profile
G F	Favorites
G L	Lists
G M	Messages
G S	Settings
G U	Go to user...

Social Media Dimensions Quick Reference

The sizes listed below are in pixels. If you do not have Photoshop. you can use Gimp or similar application to size and edit photos.

☐ Gimp
http://www.gimp.org/

Facebook Dimensions
Facebook Cover photo: 851 x 315
Facebook Profile photo: 180 x 180

Google+ Dimensions
Google+ Cover photo: 2120 x 1192
Google+ Profile photo: 270 x 270

LinkedIn Dimensions
LinkedIn Cover photo: 646 x 220
LinkedIn Profile photo: 100 x 60

Pinterest Dimensions
Pinterest Profile Photo: 160 x 165

Instagram Dimensions
Instagram Profile Photo: 110 x 110

Twitter Dimensions
Twitter Header image: 520 x 260
Twitter Profile image: 81 x 81

YouTube Dimensions
YouTube Cover Art: 2560 x 1440
YouTube Cover Art Safe Area: 1546 x 423

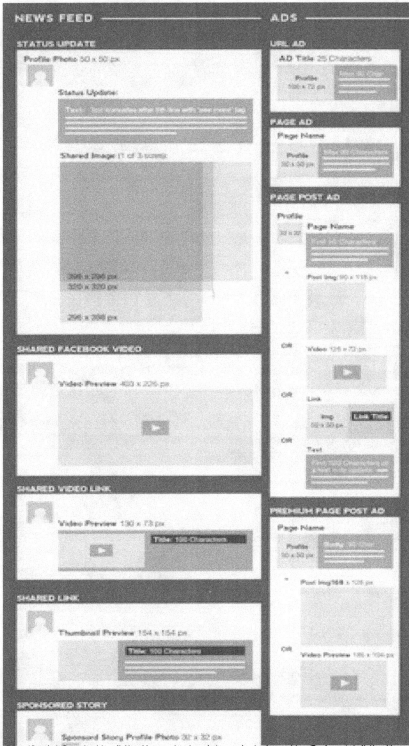

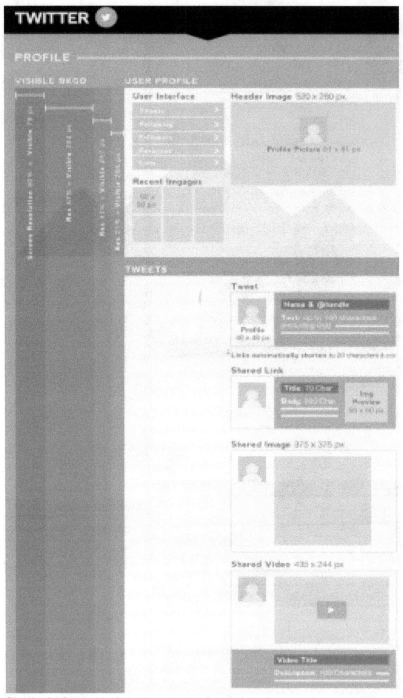

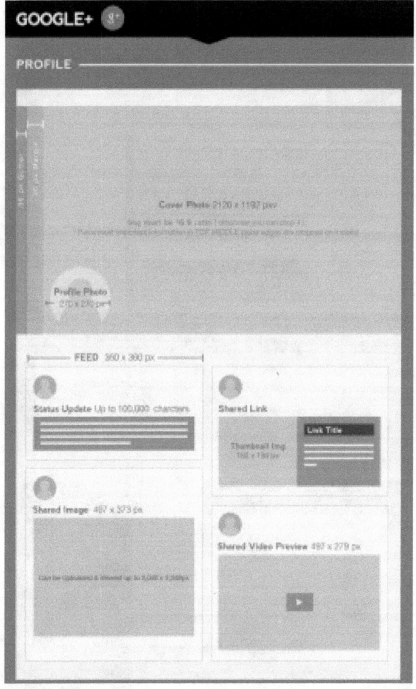

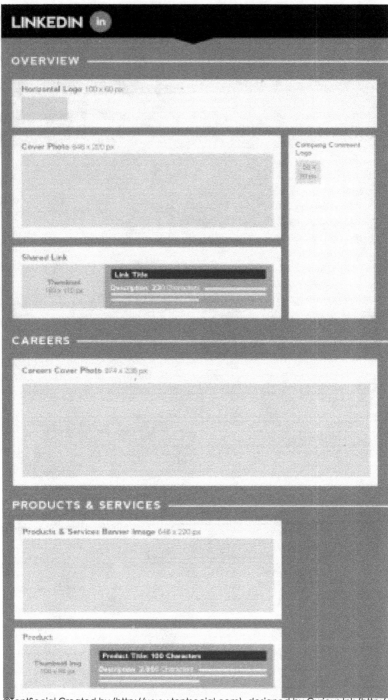

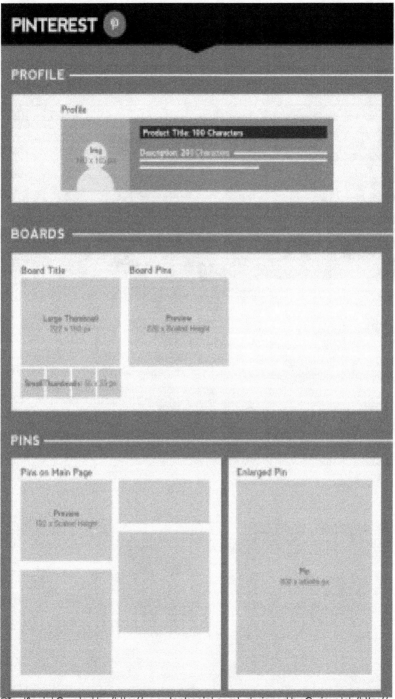

©TentSocial Created by (http://www.tentsocial.com), designed by Curious Ink (http://www.curiousink.ca)

Applications by Category

Expense Management

Facebook Contest

Facebook Homes for Sale Tab Apps

Facebook Tab Apps

Financial Organization

Group Tweeting

Homeowner & Neighborhood Information

Key Control

Location Based Apps

Marketing

Measuring and Floorplans

MLS Apps

NFC Tags

Online Reputation

Open Houses

Photographs

Pinterest Apps

Privacy Policy

Property Management

QR Code Generator

QR Code Readers

QR Code Resources

Real Estate App Builders

Real Estate CRM

Real Estate Documents

Real Estate Investment

Security

Social Media Policy

Social Media Site Name

Twitter Chats

Twitter Community Building

Twitter Dashboard Applications

Twitter Influencer Applications

Twitter Lists

Twitter Management

Twitter Polls/Surveys

Index

Websites

Credits

GRAPHICS
©Depositphotos/art1art
©Depositphotos/drizzd
©Depositphotos/kbuntu, p.4

REFERENCES
[1] http://nomadmobileguides.com/
[2]The 2012 American Express® Global Customer
Service Barometer
    http://about.americanexpress.com/news/
    docs/2012x/AXP_2012GCSB_US.pdf

Social Media Infographic
©TentSocial - The Ridiculously Exhaustive Social-
Media Dimensions Blueprint; Created by (http://tent-
social.com/), designed by Curious Ink (http://www.
curiousink.ca)